PRAYER BOOK REVISION

IN THE

CHURCH IN WALES

PRAYER BOOK REVISION

IN THE

CHURCH IN WALES

BY

EWART LEWIS, M.A.

VICAR OF LLANBLETHIAN WITH COWBRIDGE
RURAL DEAN OF COWBRIDGE

HONORARY SECRETARY OF THE STANDING LITURGICAL COMMISSION
OF THE CHURCH IN WALES

THE CHURCH IN WALES PROVINCIAL COUNCIL FOR EDUCATION,
LLANDAFF HOUSE, PENARTH, GLAMORGAN
1958

PRINTED BY
D. BROWN AND SONS, LTD., PRINTERS, COWBRIDGE, GLAM.

FOREWORD

THE Reverend E. O. T. Lewis, whose services to the Church in Wales have been known since the publication of his essay "The Church in Wales, the Catholic Faith and the Future" and his Secretaryship of the "Nation and Prayer Book" Commission, has placed us further in his debt by this study of Prayer Book Revision. I am sure that as we consider this question we would do well to place it in the context in which we find it here, and I warmly commend it to all those who are ready, as all should be, to give their minds to find how best the Church in Wales may join in the worship of Almighty God.

✠GLYN LANDAV:

14*th July*, 1958.

PREFACE

DURING this century, Prayer Book revision has become a major issue in the Anglican world. As Provinces have undertaken this work, it has often been said that their proposals must fail of their full effect unless churchpeople generally appreciate the reasons for revising the 1662 Book, and the principles upon which revised services are based.

Since 1951, when revision work began in the Church in Wales, the cry for instruction has been heard in this Province also; and this essay is a modest attempt to answer it. Besides describing the general background of revision in the Anglican Communion, I have sought to explain the machinery for revision lately set up in the Church in Wales, and the reasons for the proposals which have so far received the Governing Body's assent and authorisation from the Bench of Bishops. If some pages, and those of Section B in particular, make heavy reading, I can but beg forgiveness, and shelter behind the undoubted fact that the ecclesiastical law is a lady content with no rapid homage on the part of her pursuers.

My first and chief debt is to the Provincial Council for Education, which has sponsored publication, and to its Secretary, the Reverend D. G. Childs, who among the many offices of a long-standing friendship has given me here also invaluable criticism and material help. Several clergy and laity read the essay in typescript and commented upon it. They are the Archbishop of Wales, and the Bishops of Llandaff and Bangor; the Very Reverend Eryl S. Thomas, Chairman of the Standing Liturgical Commission; the Venerable C. Gwynne Lewis and the Venerable J. Gwynno James; the Reverend P. E. N. David; Mr. Aneirin Talfan Davies, Captain N. G. Garnons Williams, and Major and Mrs. C. G. Traherne. I thank them all for an interest which has meant the removal of many obscurities and the repair of some omissions. I am particularly grateful to the Bishop of Llandaff. He subjected the typed draft to a minute scrutiny and sent me a detailed list of criticisms, and has been good enough to write a Foreword. Together with the Reverend Alun Davies, his Secretary, and Mr. J. R. Law of the Representative Body's staff, he has also given me much help over the history of Prayer Book revision in the Church in Wales between 1920 and 1947. I would also thank the Reverend Dr. F. L. Cross, Lady Margaret Professor of Divinity in the University of Oxford, and Messrs. A. R. Mowbray, for permission to print, on page 51, the paragraph from Dr. Cross's translation of A. Baumstark's *Liturgie Comparée*. The printers, Messrs. D. Brown & Sons, Ltd., have been kindness and care itself.

I remain, nevertheless, solely responsible for the statements of fact and opinion here put forward, and for the errors and ambiguities which doubtless remain. In view of the fact that I am privileged to be a member of it, it may be well to state that this essay is in no sense an official document issued by the Standing Liturgical Commission, and that my colleagues are in no way responsible for what I have written. Throughout the Commission's life, however, the need of liturgical education has been keenly felt and often discussed : and I am proud to dedicate these pages to that body, knowing as I do how much they owe to its deliberations.

EWART LEWIS

Llanblethian.
July, 1958.

CONTENTS

IN SEPTEMBER, 1956, the Governing Body of the Church in Wales assented to the experimental use of a revised Table of Lessons and Psalms for Sundays and certain other days. In January, 1958, the Bishops of the Church in Wales, each for his own diocese, authorised the experimental use of revised services of Baptism and Confirmation. These services had received the assent of the Governing Body at its meeting in Easter Week, 1957. There have thus been submitted to the Church's judgement the first fruits of labours which have gone on continuously since the appointment of a Standing Liturgical Commission by the late Archbishop of Wales in January, 1951. This essay seeks to give some account of the background of this task, of the machinery created for its execution, and of the revisions so far approved for experimental use.

A

THE BOOK OF 1662 AND THE CASE FOR REVISING IT : REVISION IN THE ANGLICAN COMMUNION

ALTHOUGH he served her only some five years, the Church in Wales may count among her great servants William Beveridge, Bishop of St. Asaph from 1704 to 1708. Coming late in the brilliant succession of the Caroline divines, and a man as holy as he was learned, Beveridge in one of his writings thus describes the purpose of public worship. It must edify and lead us from strength to strength, from one degree of grace to another, "until at length we arrive at glory and perfection in the highest heavens, where we shall spend eternity itself in praising and adoring the most high God".[1]

In saying this, Beveridge presumably had in mind the Prayer Book of 1662, then very new, by now nearly three hundred years old. If we have known and loved that Book at all, we cannot but join hands with the generations before us in placing it among the glories of Christendom, and in confessing how soberly, beautifully, and surely, it has led countless Christians through the changes of this life to the peace of the blessed. Moreover, we will recognise with successive Lambeth Conferences that the Book of 1662 enshrines in the most authoritative form those standards of doctrine and worship which bind together the Anglican Communion as a

(1) G. W. O. Addleshaw, *The High Church Tradition*, London, 1941, p. 74.

1

whole.[2]   No careless hands must be laid upon such a treasure : and now that the work of revising the 1662 Book has begun in the Church in Wales, our faithful people have every right to ask why revision is necessary.

The 1662 Book is essentially a product of the Reformation period.   It is, so far as our part of the Church is concerned, the expression of the efforts made by the men of that time to have the Church services as well as the Scriptures in their own tongue, and to purge the Church from superstitions in doctrine, and ceremonies which had become "dark" and "dumb"[3] to most worshippers.   The principal architect of the Book was Thomas Cranmer, who became Archbishop of Canterbury under Henry VIII, and was put to death under Mary in 1556.   In a lecture delivered in commemoration of the fourth centenary of his death, Dr. Norman Sykes said : "Of Thomas Cranmer most particularly we may say with equal verity and modesty, *Si monumentum requiris, circumspice.* For his memorial is written in the largest letters in our Liturgy, Ordinal, and Articles.   Four centuries of English churchmen have nourished their corporate and private religious life upon his Collects, his Litany and his Eucharistic Office".[4]   Welsh as well as English churchmen will acknowledge the justice of that tribute.   The authority which it has acquired over the centuries, the permanent validity of the principles which guided its composition, and its chief compiler's genius for liturgical language, have endeared the 1662 Book to us as much as our brethren over the border.

Love, however, is not meant to stifle thought and criticism, above all when the matter in hand is no less a thing than the due honour of God, and the proclamation through the Church's worship of His saving acts in our Lord Jesus Christ.   Viewed against the modern world, and in the light of nearly three centuries of use, the 1662 Book will not seem to the devout and thoughtful Anglican of the 1950's the perfect instrument which Bishop Beveridge and

(2) "The Book of Common Prayer, next to the Bible itself, is the authoritative standard of the doctrine of the Anglican Communion"; (Lambeth Conference Encyclical Letter, 1897).   *Cf.* Resolution 78 of the 1948 Conference : "The Conference holds that the Book of Common Prayer has been, and is, so strong a bond of unity throughout the whole Anglican Communion that great care must be taken to ensure that revisions of the Book shall be in accordance with the doctrine and accepted liturgical worship of the Anglican Communion".

(3) Prayer Book Preface, *Of Ceremonies.*

(4) *Thomas Cranmer,* 1489-1556.   *Three commemorative lectures delivered in Lambeth Palace* : Church Information Board, London, p. 25.

his contemporaries thought it to be. Let us consider some of the issues involved in its continued use.

(1) Language. We have already said that Cranmer's English is one of the chief glories of Anglicanism. One of the most delicate problems facing revisers of the 1662 Book is how to change it without loss either of its dignity and rhythm, or of the doctrinal content in which it is so rich. But this does not alter the fact that not a few words used by Cranmer have greatly changed their meaning in the centuries between him and ourselves, and that some of the idioms beloved of sixteenth-century English perplex their modern hearers. Time after time, Cranmer's English presents a real "problem of communication" to faithful churchpeople in this age, let alone the chance worshipper or the person seeking for spiritual truth in an era of doubt.[5]

The "problem of communication" is further complicated for us in this Province by our use of the Welsh as well as the English version of the 1662 Book. The Welsh version stems back to the translation of the 1552 English Book made by William Salesbury and Bishop Richard Davies, and published in May, 1567.[6] Its own merits, and its use by generation of Welsh-speaking churchpeople, have won for this version also a deep attachment. But by now, it too shows signs of age. Many of its words have become obsolete or difficult to understand, and many of its sentences and turns of speech sound clumsy to the Welsh-speaking person of today. Since the end of last century, the study of Welsh grammar and philology have made great strides : and everything now written in Welsh has to conform to the canons of orthography established in that period. The orthography of the Welsh version of 1662, however, remains substantially that of the edition of 1841. It is felt that these deficiencies are a considerable stumbling-block to the Church's mission in the Welsh-speaking areas of Wales.

(2) Rubrics. Churchmen are familiar with the directions on order, ceremonial, and other matters found printed in italics on most pages of the 1662 Book. The passage of time has much affected the force of many rubrics. Some have become obsolete, others are vague or not sufficiently comprehensive to cover modern practice

---

(5) For a valuable and stimulating study of Cranmer and other religious writers of his age as stylists, *cf.* C. S. Lewis, *English Literature in the Sixteenth Century*, Oxford, 1954, pp. 157-221.

(6) See Melville Richards and Glanmor Williams (editors), *Llyfr Gweddi Gyffredin 1567*, Cardiff, 1953: with an introduction.

and individual circumstances. Reporting as long ago as 1906, the Royal Commission on Ecclesiastical Discipline gave a list of practices all familiar to churchpeople, but all illegal on a strict construction of the rubrics as they stand. The list included hymn-singing at services, addresses at Confirmations, giving out notices otherwise than after the Nicene Creed, using prayers other than those provided after the Third Collect, celebrating the Holy Communion more than once on any day, and celebrating without a sermon or homily[7]. As the Report itself says, "the law of public worship in the Church of England is too narrow for the religious life of the present generation. It needlessly condemns much which a great section of Churchpeople, including many of her most devoted members, value" . . . [8] What was true in 1906 is even more true today, nor is it only a question of the law needlessly condemning useful things. As with the State, so with the Church the law governing it is itself brought into contempt when it is either obsolete or operates harshly in existing circumstances. Principle, therefore, as well as practical requirements dictate a revision of the 1662 rubrics.

(3) Political and Social Changes. The 1662 Book throughout reflects the political and social conditions of the Tudor and Stuart periods. British life has seen profound changes in the centuries since. While readily admitting that it is a Christian duty to pray for rulers and that the Prayer Book should provide for its performance, many churchmen of today would question whether it is right to go on using forms of prayer for those in authority which at some points suggest that we are still in the era of the Divine Right of Kings; and whether, for example, the first prayer for the Queen in the Communion Office does not sound somewhat exaggerated on the lips of a person living under a constitutional monarch and a Parliament freely elected by the people. Again, the social conditions presupposed by the 1662 Book are by no means those of today. In the Tudor and Stuart eras, England and Wales were still generally Christian, and still in the main consisted of small towns, villages, or farming communities in which clergy and people could know each other closely. By now, though such communities remain,

(7) See *Liturgy and Worship*, London, 1932, p. 604, note 2. For an account of this important Commission and Its Report, see G. K. A. Bell, *Randall Davidson*, second edition, London, 1938, ch. 25, pp. 454-473.

(8) Cd. 3040, 1906, §399. *Cf.* Bell, *op. cit.* p. 471.

there exist side by side with them vast urban and industrial districts, Lewis Mumford's "Coketown" or "Megalopolis".[9] In such places, life has become not merely impersonal, but also gravely withdrawn from the influence of the Christian religon.

The 1662 Book, it is fair to say, assumes that everyone using it knows the elements of Christianity and has some understanding of the liturgical way of worship which church services follow. It would be dangerous to make either assumption in our age. The vast changes which we have seen have affected the usefulness of 1662 in another way. As liturgical knowledge grows, and actual revision of existing forms has brought experience, the modern age is perhaps more chary than its immediate predecessors of multiplying in the public worship of the Church, which is the corporate act of the faithful and not a gathering together of individual aspirations, the numbers of prayers referring to particular circumstances, persons or institutions. Yet, the universal use, authorised or not, of occasional prayers drawn from all kinds of sources amply proves the fact that the Occasional Prayers and Thanksgivings provided in 1662 are far from reflecting the life of modern Britain in all its complexity and variety. So far as Wales is concerned, apart from the permission to translate the Prayer Book into the Welsh language, and the Black-Letter Day given to St. David in the Calendar, little if anything in 1662 recognises our existence as a distinct nation possessing traditions of our own, and national institutions, which could and should be prayed for from time to time in the services of the Church. Although the Church in Wales has now been disestablished for nearly forty years and is a self-governing Province of the Anglican Communion, she continues to use a Prayer Book bearing on its title-page the words "according to the use of the Church of England" : and there is no need to labour the anomaly of that situation.[10]

(9) See his *Culture of Cities*, London, 1938, chs. 3 and 4, pp.143-299.

(10) The Report of the "Nation and Prayer Book" Commission, presented to the Governing Body of the Church in Wales in September, 1949, gives on pp. 75-77 a fuller account of the difficulties involved in the use of 1662 in modern Wales. The Representative Body of the Church in Wales was requested to make the Report generally available. The English version is now exhausted, but copies of the Welsh version, price 1/-, may still be obtained on application to the Representative Body of the Church in Wales, 39 Cathedral Road, Cardiff.

(4) The Reformation and the Progress of Historical, Theological and Liturgical Studies

So far, we have discussed the more practical issues raised by the continued use of 1662. But intellectual issues are involved as well, and some understanding of these is vital if the question of Prayer Book revision is to be fairly considered.

On any showing, the Reformation was one of the mighty turning-points in the history of the world. It has been rightly observed that the tensions underlying its controversies still await their reconciliation in the life of the Anglican Communion. Evangelicals continue to stress the prophetic element in the Christian faith, and Christ's appeal to the conscience of the individual believer. Catholics on their side stress the divine origin and universality of the Church, the continuity of her ministry, doctrine, and worship from Apostolic times, and the importance of membership of Christ's Body in its ordered life of prayer, Word, and Sacrament. All these matters were fiercely debated at the Reformation. And the Anglican Communion still numbers among its adherents those who unreservedly admire the achievements of the Reformation, or condemn it as the greatest disaster which has ever befallen the Christian world. When one considers how great was the heat of the Reformation controversies, it is indeed wonderful that the 1662 Book preserved the "proportion of faith" as well as it did.

Extreme partisanship never serves the cause of truth in the long run if its persistence, after controversy has made clear the common ground between the opposing parties, results in the prevention of progress and mutual understanding. So far as Prayer Book revision is concerned, the progress of historical, theological, and liturgical studies since the Reformation has done much to convince fair-minded persons that 1662 is not sacrosanct or perfect, great achievement that it is; and has served to warn us that if 1662 is to be revised, this must not be done to suit the views either of liberal humanism or of a rigid papalism.

To take, first, the progress of historical studies. Dr. Butterfield's *Man on His Past* is an impressive reminder of the debt which the world owes to the 17th and 18th century scholars whose work established scientific and impartial methods of historical enquiry.[11] Here and abroad these methods have been applied to the history of the Reformation. If the result has served to underline the zeal of the great Reformers, it has also shown that they were very much men of their time, subject to its prejudices and intellectual limitations. Further, the Reformation, to quote Sir Maurice Powicke's description of its English career, was "an act of State" in which the will of princes played a leading role, and with which was mixed the greed of the nobility and the rising mercantile classes, both anxious to seize the possessions of the Church.[12] Four hundred years on, Anglicans still have a duty to be thankful for the Scriptures and Church services in their own tongue, for the purging of the Church from many superstitions and abuses, and for all the other ideals for which the Reformers fought. But the knowledge we now have makes it no longer possible to regard the Reformation as a religious crusade undefiled by human sin or error.

Theology as well as history has made progress. The opening decades of the 19th century saw the emergence of that group of Christian soldiers and thinkers which is called the "Tübingen School". This group applied to the Bible the critical disciplines becoming popular among the historians, and launched that intense study of the Biblical text, and of the historical and other problems posed by the different parts of Scripture, which reached its fine flower in England in the work of Lightfoot, Westcott, and Hort. This phase in Biblical studies was accompanied by much liberalism, a good deal of it destructive of Christian faith, among theologians. This produced its inevitable reaction, and recent times have seen the rise of what is called "Biblical Theology". Sir Edwyn Hoskyns was the outstanding representative of this school in England, and his *Riddle of the New Testament* and his unfinished commentary on

(11) Cambridge, 1955.

(12) *The Reformation in England*, Oxford, 1941, p. 1. Originally one of the essays in the fourth volume of Edward Eyre's *European Civilisation: its Origin and Development* (Oxford, 1936), this book, the work of a great medievalist, is to be commended to anyone wishing to see the Reformation in the light of modern scholarship. By his *Bywyd a Gwaith yr Esgob Richard Davies* (Cardiff, 1953), and other writings, Professor Glanmor Wllliams of University College Swansea, has thrown much light on the progress of the Reformation in Wales; the general study of this period of Welsh history which he is writing is eagerly awaited.

St. John have had an immense influence.[13] Biblical theologians are on the whole mindful of the benefits of critical methods as applied to the study of the Scriptures. But they emphasise that concentration on the details of Biblical scholarship must not produce a refusal to look at the Bible as a whole. Variegated as its contents are, it has a unity of theme and purpose as the record of God's dealings with the world from its creation to the refounding of His Church in Our Lord Jesus Christ. The record points back to Adam and the Fall, and forward to that consummation when God will be "all in all". As the ancient saying has it, "the New Testament is hidden in the Old, the Old is revealed in the New" : and the full glory and wisdom of the Divine plan for the world is obscured if one part of the Bible record of it is treated in isolation from others.[14]

Closely connected with the developments in Biblical study are those in the study of the Christian Fathers and the history of the primitive Church. The Fathers were above all else men steeped in Scripture. The 19th century made great contributions to the study of them. This work has continued into our own age. If perhaps it is not so obvious here at home—though we too have had distinguished patristic scholars like C. H. Turner, G. L. Prestige, Darwell Stone, E. Evans, and F. L. Cross—the work of G. Morin, A. Wilmart, H. de Lubac, Emil Mersch, J. de Ghellinck, and many others make it plain that an immense revival of patristic studies is going on in France and other parts of the Continent.[15]

We must also note the continuing attempt to reconcile the Christian revelation and philosophy. E. L. Mascall here, and E. Gilson and Jacques Maritain in France, are prominent advocates of "Neo-Thomism". They would defend the right of human reason to enquire into revealed truth : and arguing that the authentic

(13) E. C. Hoskyns and F. N. Davey ; *The Riddle of the New Testament*, revised edition, London, 1936 : F. N. Davey (editor); E. C. Hoskyns, *The Fourth Gospel*, revised edition, London, 1947.

(14) For a good general account of these movements in Biblical study see C. H. Dodd, *The Bible Today*, Cambridge, 1941; *cf.* H. H. Rowley, *The Relevance of the Bible*, London, 1941.

(15) No general survey of modern trends in patristic studies seems to have been published in England. But the two volumes of J. Quasten's *Patrology*, published in English at Utrecht in 1950 and 1953, cover the period up to the Council of Nicea (325 A.D.), in the light of recent researches.

tradition of Christian philosophy is contained in the Fathers and Schoolmen, they seek to apply their categories of thought to the statement of Christian truth in this age. In this, they are at variance with Christian thinkers who look for light from later philosophical systems, and in total discord with Karl Barth and his followers, who maintain the complete transcendence of God, and the worthlessness of man's reason in consequence of the Fall.[16]

To turn now to strictly liturgical scholarship. As is shown by the *Rationale divinorum officiorum* of Durandus of Mende, the medieval period was not without men interested in the history of Christian worship. But the scientific study of liturgies as we know it today did not begin till the 17th and early 18th centuries. This is the period of the great collections of Mabillon, Martène, Gavanti, Tomassi, and Renaudot; and scholars like F. Cabrol and H. Leclercq have worked on a comparable scale nearer our own time. The Tractarian Movement stimulated interest in liturgiology among Anglicans. W. Maskell, J. M. Neale and G. H. Forbes in the last century, and F. E. Brightman, W. H. Frere, J. H. Srawley, and E. C. Ratcliff in this, are names worthy to stand with L. Duchesne, E. Bishop, J. A. Jungmann, A. Baumstark and other prominent Roman liturgiologists of recent times. The "Alcuin Club" and the "Henry Bradshaw Society" have both been reponsible for an impressive series of publications. All this work has thrown an immense amount of light on the development of Christian worship, and the labour and patience which have gone to it are one of the great glories of European learning.[17]

We have tried to trace the main outlines of a vast movement in Christian thought and scholarship. In it, in our own times, what is called the "Liturgical Movement" has played a leading part. The origins of this movement are to be found in the Roman Catholic Church. Its nineteenth century forerunner was the French Benedictine P. L. P. Guéranger. In 1833, he opened the priory of Solesmes. His voluminous and popularly written books on

(16) See J. V. L. Casserley, *The Christian in Philosophy*, London, 1949.

(17) No history of liturgical scholarship exists in English. See the articles on individual liturgiologists in F. L. Cross (editor) , *The Oxford Dictionary of the Christian Church*, London, 1957, and the bibliographies attached. See also the valuable appendix to L. Bouyer, *Life and Liturgy*, London, 1956, pp. 272-281.

liturgical questions were widely read. In 1903, Pius X became Pope. His reform of the Breviary or daily office book of the Roman Church was followed by decrees on sacred music and frequent communion. These acts by authority gave the Liturgical Movement an immense impetus. The Benedictines have done much to foster it. With Solesmes, their abbeys at Maredsous and Mont César in Belgium and at Maria Laach in Germany have by now been for many years its leading centres : and I. Herwegen, L. Beauduin, G. Laporta and B. Capelle among Benedictines, together with the Augustinian P. Parsch, stand out among its Continental advocates. The movement has spread widely in Europe, and gains ground, though slowly, in America.

In Great Britain, the Movement does not seem so far to count for a great deal among Roman Catholics, though enterprising publishers of their communion have published several translations of books written by its Continental supporters. In its issue of Easter, 1958, *Les Questiones Liturgiques et Paroissiales*, a well-known periodical published at Mont César, surveyed country by country recent liturgical activities and publications ; it was interesting to note that Ireland received a short paragraph, but not England. In matters of this kind, the Roman hierarchy here is markedly conservative, and this fact no doubt tells. As for our own Church, its adoption of the vernacular at the Reformation secured at one stroke one of the chief objects in which the Liturgical Movement is interested. But we had to wait for the Tractarian movement of last century before there was advance in another cardinal matter, the understanding of the Eucharist. As we have said, Tractarianism stimulated liturgical study among Anglicans. It also produced in parish after parish more frequent celebrations of the Holy Communion, and more frequent acts of communion by individuals. Someone might profitably examine the influence upon each other, if any, of the Tractarians and the nineteenth century forerunners of the Liturgical Movement. Whatever is the truth about this, our long-standing use of the vernacular, and the return to more frequent communion secured by the Tractarians, had prepared the ground to an appreciable extent when in 1935, through his book *Liturgy and Society*, A. G. Hebert introduced the modern Liturgical Movement to Anglicans at large. In 1943, there appeared *The Shape of the Liturgy*, the massive and fascinating book in which G. Dix sought to explain the structure of the Eucharist in the primitive Church, and the distortions of practice and doctrine which later ages imposed upon it. Both books have had important results; the increasing popularity of the "Parish Communion", and the activities of the "Parish and People" movement, are the chief outward signs of their influence.

What are the aims of the Liturgical Movement? During the Middle Ages, infrequent communion became more and more the rule. Church services, moreover, were in a language which few could follow. Christian worship became distorted because the role of the priesthood in it was unduly magnified, and because the laity could not take an intelligent part in it. Left to tell their beads or to use such vernacular manuals of devotion as were available, the faithful became more and more pietistic and self-centred in their approach to worship. The activities of the Reformers, and the spiritual revival which the Council of Trent initiated in the Roman Church, were not successful in overcoming this individualism. As against it, the Liturgical Movement insists that the worship of the Church is the offering to God in every place of the whole of human life. In this offering, individual personality and aspirations are not obliterated, but are enlarged and enriched because they become part of the offering of the Body of Christ. The worship of the Church, then, properly understood, is corporate and all-inclusive; and its crown and climax is the Holy Communion with frequent reception of the Sacrament. For the realisation of these principles, the Liturgical Movement uses a variety of means. By advocating a greater use of the vernacular, it seeks to do in the Roman Church what was done for Anglicanism in the 16th century. It seeks the fuller use or revival of truly significant ceremonies, for example the ancient custom of celebrating facing the people, and the offering by the people of the bread and wine for the Eucharist in such a way as to make it plain that it is the offering by the whole congregation of its whole life. Again, the Movement is eager for manuals which will lead the laity to be active participants in services rather than passive attendants at them. In these and other ways does it strive to develop the full Christian life of prayer and service, in which the devotions of the private chamber find their due complement in a public worship which is corporate and intelligent, and builds up the faithful, "high and low, rich and poor, one with another" into their Lord and Head, Jesus Christ. On the Continent, the Liturgical Movement has stimulated a vast amount of practical experiment, especially in parishes touched by the ideals of the "Mission de Paris". We may compare in our own Communion ventures such as those at Parson Cross, Sheffield, and at Halton. Equally important, the movement has inspired a vast number of theological and liturgical studies, much periodical writing, and a growing number of books in which the work of theologians and liturgiologists is directly related to the daily worship of the Church and individual devotion. The Liturgical Movement no doubt has its exaggerations and misguided enthusiasms, and it has not lacked its clashes with authority. But that it is one of the significant forces in modern Christianity, and that its ideas and findings are vital for liturgical progress, are both undoubted facts.[18]

We must now attempt to sum up the results of all this study in its bearing upon the question of Prayer Book revision.

First, the historians. Their work has undoubtedly enabled us to see the Reformation and its controveries in a more sober light, and as a period in which Christian idealism lived side by side with human prejudice and self-interest as much as in any era of the Church's history. Though they are far from having abolished it, the historians have done much to lessen that strong hostility to Prayer Book revision, ranging from sincere conviction to mere intransigence, which was very common, even among educated churchpeople, in previous generations.

Second, the theologians. No more than, indeed even less than, history, can theology claim to have reached final conclusions. When the theologian has done all, there remain much of God's riches which are unsearchable, and much in His ways past finding out. Yet, if we survey the work done in this age by biblical and patristic scholars and philosophical theologians, we may justly claim for it a wholeness of view, and an insight into particular areas of Christian

---

(18) For an excellent short account of the Liturgical Movement, see J. H. Srawley, *The Liturgical Movement : Its Origin and Growth*, Alcuin Club Tracts XXVII, London, 1954. A fuller and most valuable study is E. B. Koenker, *The Liturgical Renaissance in the Roman Catholic Church*, Chicago and Cambridge, 1954. See also A. G. Hebert (editor), *The Parish Communion*, London, 1937. For a survey of the Movement in Welsh, see O. G. Rees, "Y Mudiad Litwrgiaidd," in *Diwinyddiaeth* (the periodical of the theological section of the Guild of Graduates of the University of Wales), July 1956, pp. 36-41. *Cf. Province*, Christmas, 1953, pp. 256-263; Easter 1954, pp. 13-19; Summer 1954, pp. 52-59; and Autumn, 1954, pp. 95-103, for a study of parish experiments in the Church of France influenced by the Movement.

truth, which the 16th and 17th centuries often attained only in part or not at all. As will be explained at greater length in the third section of this essay, we have by now reached a more balanced view of human nature and sinfulness, and of man's destiny at God's hands, than the Reformers did. The great problem of Time and Eternity, and that part of the Christian revelation which points its followers towards the final consummation of all things in Jesus Christ, have in our day received searching and profound treatment which has all but set up a new dimension of Christian thought. Again, biblical and patristic scholars have combined to give us a richer understanding of the Church, divine in her origins, and the Body of Christ whose members are the blessed in Heaven as well as her faithful who are still pilgrims on earth. The theology of the Ministry and Sacraments has also received attention. Recent work here and abroad on such thorny questions as the nature of the Eucharistic Sacrifice and of Christ's Presence in the Sacrament offers a firmer prospect of agreement between Catholic and Protestant standpoints than we have seen hitherto. At the beginning of this essay, we admitted that the 1662 Book is the classic statement of the Anglican position. We must not forget, either, that the mind of man is fallible, and that what seemed a theological triumph at the time can eventually prove to have been a mere surrender to some passing fashion of thought. Even so, the work of theologians in recent years forces us to ask whether 1662 does not, in places, require linguistic and other changes which will make it a more complete embodiment of the Church's faith than it now is.[19]

Third, the liturgiologists and the influence of the Liturgical Movement. The learned researches and practical experiments here in view have had a two-fold result. In the first place, the Church today possesses a fuller understanding of the principles underlying her worship, and an incomparably better knowledge of its development down the centuries, than the Reformers did. In the second place, liturgical scholarship has brought home to us very clearly how much of value was lost to our own Church in the course of the developments which followed the first Prayer Book of 1549. At the Reformation, much indeed had to be done to simplify

(19) Since this paragraph was written, there has appeared (London 1958), E. L. Mascall's *The Recovery of Unity*. It treats admirably of recent developments in theological discussion: and chs. 5 and 6 ("The Rediscovery of the Liturgy"), have much that is vital for Prayer Book revision.

the rules governing public worship, to remove or amend those parts of the existing services whose wording countenanced false or exaggerated doctrine, and to cut down over-elaborate or pointless ceremonial. Yet, in the light of modern knowledge, it may well be asked whether the pruning did not go too far, and whether much useful liturgical provision, and not a few ceremonies which had meaning and were free from superstition, were not needlessly sacrificed. It is this feeling which has produced the plea for enrichment of the 1662 Book often made by advocates of revision. Many are dissatisfied with the limitation of Proper Prefaces to the Great Festivals. Many chafe at a provision of Collects, Epistles, and Gospels which covers only the feasts of Our Lord and the New Testament Saints and drives them to this or that unauthorised source if they wish to commemorate the lesser Saints in the Calendar. The same deficiency is felt over the Rogation days, the Ember seasons, and the forty days of Lent : and although the modern tendency is to favour a severe limitation of Octaves, it is agreed that the Octaves of a few Great Feasts should be duly observed. It is likewise felt that the Occasional Offices, dealing as they do with the great turning-points in human life and therefore possessing a special appeal, call for enrichment, by ceremonial and by additional provision, which would make their meaning clearer and make them more abundant sources of Divine grace and consolation to their recipients. The same considerations move those who would like to see a revival of the traditional ceremonial connected with Holy Week, with the Rogation days and Plough Sunday and Lammastide, or with Festival days such as the Purification of the Blessed Virgin. They appeal not only to ancient custom, but to the undoubted fact that this is an age in which people are educated by the eye as much as the ear. Few persons familiar with the question would deny the desirability of enrichment, provided we avoid such a degree of it as would put us back amid the complications and minutiae of medieval worship.

Such are the main considerations and forces which have made the question of Prayer Book revision a vital one in this age. The Anglican Communion has already seen a great deal of work done.[20] Let us summarize some of the results.

(a) **England.** In November 1906, following upon the Report of the Royal Commission on Ecclesiastical Discipline, Letters of Business setting on foot the work of Prayer Book revision issued to the Convocations. The result was the "Deposited Book", commonly known as the 1928 Book. The circumstances surrounding its rejection are more fully discussed in the next section of this essay. Since July 1929, the general policy of the English Bishops has been to countenance such additions to, or deviations from, 1662 as the 1928 Book proposed. Revision work was resumed in 1954, when the Archbishops of Canterbury and York, at the request of the Convocations, set up a Liturgical Commission. No results of its work in the form of revised services have yet appeared. But the Commission has prepared for the Lambeth Conference, 1958, a most valuable Report published under the title *Prayer Book Revision in the Church of England*. Beginning with a discussion of the Reformers' aims, the Report goes on to discuss events leading up to the 1928 Book, the reasons for its rejection, and its present use. Next, it gives a striking account of the theological and other developments affecting Prayer Book Revision since 1928, and follows this with a formulation of the principles which should guide future work. Finally, the Report discusses the 1662 Book as a bond of unity and standard of doctrine in the Anglican Communion. Everyone interested in the subject should read this document.[21]

(b) **Scotland.** Though not accepted, the Book of 1637 which Laud attempted to impose upon Scotland kept alive the

(20) The following survey is based, in the first place, on *Liturgy and Worship*, pp. 783-797 : *cf*. pp. 813-833. Much of this material is fully summarised in Appendix E of the "Nation and Prayer Book" Report, pp. 92-98. The matter in *Liturgy and Worship* does not go beyond 1932 : and the sources for statements on later developments are indicated as they occur.

(21) *Prayer Book Revision in the Church of England* (L.C. 1958/2), London, 1957.

memory of the Eucharistic rite of 1549, upon which the 1637 Book largely drew : and this fact eventually influenced revision in Scotland itself, and in America and South Africa. Up till 1909, when revision began, the 1662 Book was that used by the great majority of Scots Episcopalians. A Committee appointed by the Bishops submitted its work in stages to the Provincial Synod, till finally, in March 1929, the Synod authorised a new Book as an alternative to 1662. The Synod also allowed the use of the 1637 Communion Office, and, under certain conditions, that of 1928. The 1929 Book has won high praise. To quote one verdict upon it, it is "clearly the best of the Anglican Prayer Books : it draws freely on the rich material provided by the long English debates and is also strongly national, especially as regards the Eucharistic Liturgy and the Calendar."[22]

(c) **Ireland.** The 1662 Book, adopted by the Irish Convocation at the time of its publication, remained in use up to 1878, when, following Disestablishment seven years earlier, the first revised Book was adopted. In 1909, the General Synod decided to consider such alterations as would not affect doctrine or the ritual Canons. The second revised Book came into force in 1927. As may be imagined, the religious position in Ireland imposed an extremely conservative character on the Irish revision : and though it has several points of interest, it has been for the most part concerned with re-arranging the order of the Book's contents and with providing a certain amount of additional material. Note ought to be taken, however, of the revision of the Psalter in this Book. In 1913, the Archbishops of Canterbury and York set up a Committee to report on this question. For various reasons, the Committee's findings were not much acted upon in England. But the Irish and American revisions have drawn largely upon them, with good results.

(d) **America.** Revision here has a long history of much interest. 1776 saw the Declaration of Independence, and in 1784 Dr. Seabury was consecrated as the first American Bishop at Aberdeen. There followed a period of much revision activity

(22) W. K. L. Clarke in *Liturgy and Worship*, p. 792.

marked by some confusion over matters of principle, and chiefly noteworthy for the adoption, in 1789, of the Scottish form of Consecration Prayer ; the Athanasian Creed was omitted in the same year, and its exclusion has continued. The first revision was completed in 1804. In 1892 a second revision, consisting mostly of verbal changes, was adopted. In 1913, a Commission was set up to consider the revision and enrichment of the Prayer Book. Its labours produced the third revision of 1928. As the introduction of new matter had been disallowed since 1925 in order to secure the Book's adoption in 1928, and as this meant that several features in the English and Scottish revisions could not be considered for incorporation in the 1928 American Book, it was decided to continue the life of the body which had compiled that Book, and to reconstitute it as a Standing Liturgical Commission. The duties of the Commission are to preserve materials for revision already accumulated, and to consider any suggestions put to it by the General Convention, dioceses, or individuals. The Commission works on the principle that further revision cannot be undertaken until there has been a period for study and discussion, so that when another revision is launched, it may proceed in an atmosphere of understanding and occupy less of the General Convention's time. In 1949, the Convention authorised the Commission to publish its findings in a series of Prayer Book Studies. Between 1950 and 1953, five of these Studies appeared, treating of Baptism and Confirmation, the Liturgical Lectionary, the Ministry to the Sick, the Holy Communion, and the Litany. Each Study contains a revised form not authorised for public use, but submitted for discussion. The principle governing the issue of these Studies, and their valuable contents, alike deserve the serious consideration of Anglican revisers.[23]

(e) **Canada.** The movement for revision may be said to begin in 1896, and its early stages were abortive. But in 1911, the work

(23) *The Prayer Book Studies* are published by the Church Pension Fund, New York, and are readily available in this country. See the Preface to the first volume for an authoritative account of recent developments in Prayer Book revision in America.

began in earnest, a comprehensive form of enquiry being sent out to all clergy and all lay members of the General Synod. Final approval was given to the revised Book in 1921, and it came into use at Easter, 1922. Though it contains much amendment of rubrics, and a considerable amount of new matter, the Book on the whole is conservative in tone, and the Communion service is hardly touched. Following the General Synod of 1943, there was set up a "Committee for the Revision of the Prayer Book". This Committee has done its work through sub-committees in different parts of Canada, whose work was revised by a "Central Revision Sub-Committee". The Draft Prayer Book of 1955, presented to General Synod in September of that year, is the fruit of these labours; parts of it had been approved for permissive use at earlier Synods. It goes a good deal further in innovation than the 1918 Book. The Order of Holy Communion approximates more to 1549 lines, the language of the Psalter has received a good deal of correction, and the Collects, Epistles, and Gospels owe much to the study of them made by Archbishop Carrington of Quebec. Other noteworthy features are the changes made in the Occasional Offices, the reduction of prefatory matter, and the re-arrangement of the Book's contents.[24]

(f) **South Africa.** The work has been done by Episcopal Synod, which put out a number of tentative editions with requests for comments. Ratification has been by Provincial Synod, meeting every five years. An alternative Order of Holy Communion received final approval in 1929; this is much influenced by 1549. A complete revised Book was issued by Provincial Synod in 1954 as an alternative to 1662. A few months after its appearance, the Dean of George severely criticised some of its characteristics, accusing it of humanism and sentimentalism and incoherent theology, and commenting adversely on the fact that most of it had been compiled by the Bishops unassisted. His observations had some force, but by no means vitiate the value of the Book. For revision of the

---

(24) See the Preface to the 1955 Draft Book. *Cf.* R. L. Seaborn in *Theology*, July, 1955, pp. 262-264.

Calendar, the Collects, Epistles and Gospels, and the Occasional Offices, for rubrical revision, and in many other ways, the new South Africa Book is a profitable quarry. And no less than other revised Books does it keep in view the special needs of the country for which it was composed.[25]

(g) **India.** In 1945, the Episcopal Synod of the Church of India, Burma and Ceylon (Pakistan has been added to this title since) asked the Liturgical Committee of that Church to consider and report upon the preparation of a Prayer Book for the Province. In October, 1951, the Synod considered the Committee's proposals, and with some amendments authorised their publication under the title "A Proposed Prayer Book . . . authorised by the Episcopal Synod . . . in 1951". In his Foreword, the Metropolitan explains that before this Book can become the Prayer Book of the Province, two consecutive sessions of the General Council of the Province must have discussed and accepted it; and that even then, 1662 in its entirety will continue to be a legal alternative. Meanwhile, the Book is issued for study, and the Metropolitan expresses the hope that since the Episcopal Synod has authorised the public use of the forms contained in it, the Book will be extensively used in churches. The Book was published, in English, in January 1953. The fact that it is a volume of 931 pages will sufficiently indicate the amount and variety of the matter contained in it. Several diocesan liturgical committees considered it. On receiving their reports in January 1955, the Synod decided to prepare a new draft Prayer Book for presentation to the General Council in January 1956. This draft omitted the Appendices of the 1951 Book and other matter; and it was proposed that most of the omitted portions, after further consideration, should be published in a supplementary volume. The draft also made several alterations and omissions in deference to the evangelical point of view, and effected several practical and literary improvements. At General Council, the draft was withdrawn, chiefly, it seems because evangelical members did not think it went far enough

(25) F. C. Synge, *Theology*, February, 1955, pp. 57-8. *Cf.* the spirited rejoinder by W. H. T. Gahan, *ibid.*, May, 1955, pp. 189-191.

to meet them, and also because it was felt that the relevant Canons were not clear on procedure. It was nevertheless decided that the draft be printed and submitted to the diocesan councils. Meanwhile, on 25th February, 1955, the Archbishop of Canterbury had written to the Metropolitan a letter asking for information on Prayer Book revision for the Lambeth Conference, 1958. The Metropolitan set up a Select Committee to deal with this matter. By December 1956, the Committee had prepared a Report which has now been published as one of the Reports of the Lambeth Conference, under the title *Principles of Prayer Book Revision*. Most of this extremely impressive document consists of a review of revisions already made in the Anglican Communion. It then examines the proposals before its own Church, and couples with this a survey of opinion on liturgical matters in India. Finally, the Report discusses developments in the Church of South India, with particular attention to the "Service of the Lord's Supper or the Holy Eucharist" authorised for optional use on any occasion by the Synod of that Church in January, 1954. *Principles of Prayer Book Revision* is fully worthy to stand with the English Report already discussed, and richly repays close consideration.[26]

This summary of events, will have shown that the situation in this Province is confused, and future prospects of Prayer Book revision uncertain. The Lambeth Report admits that neither of the extreme wings of opinion is at all enthusiastic for revision. On the other hand, the field is free for experiment. When it became an autonomous Province in 1930, the Church of India, Burma, and Ceylon formally stated in its Canons that one of its aims was "to work towards the development of worship congenial to the nature of the Indian races", and that in pursuance of this aim it wished "to give opportunities for great liberty in experiment".[27] The 1951 Book ought to

[26] *Principles of Prayer Book Revision* (LC 1958/3), London, 1957. Pp. 67-99, and 102-103, give a full account of the present liturgical situation in the Church of India, and in the Church of South India. *Cf.* the Preface to the 1951 Book, and the informative article by J. D. M. Stuart, *Theology*, October, 1956, pp. 404-408. L. Bouyer has an interesting and appreciative discussion of the South Indian Eucharistic Office in *Theology*, January, 1956, pp. 3-7.

[27] *Principles*, p. 66.

give ample scope for experiment at home and discussion elsewhere. It draws freely on other revisions. It is original in its treatment of Fasting and Abstinence. To ensure recognition of that Sacrament's equal dignity, the services of Baptism come immediately before the Holy Communion. The Confirmation service lays special stress on witness. The Holy Communion has a Prayer of Consecration which follows the Eastern tradition of an Invocation of the Holy Spirit; a special "Liturgy for India" is also provided. Many of the new Collects have a marked missionary emphasis. The strict penitential discipline characteristic of many dioceses in the Province finds expression in various ways. All in all, this revision also is not to be overlooked.

This account of the situation in different parts of the Anglican Communion has been compiled from the information available to the writer. He would be the first to admit that it leaves large areas of the Anglican Communion uncovered. It is, in fact, a most difficult matter to obtain up-to-date information about what is happening over Prayer Book revision in the different Provinces. At the Lambeth Conference, 1958, one of the main matters to be discussed will be that of revision. One hopes that one of the chief results of this drawing of the threads together will be a printed account which will enable us to see the movement for the revision of 1662 as a whole, and enlighten our ignorance on many points connected with it. Meanwhile, what has been said in this study may be sufficient to show members of the Church in Wales that in embarking in our turn on a revision of 1662, we are not doing something novel or revolutionary, but are joining a great stream of study and experiment which will enrich the life of the whole Anglican Communion for years to come.

B

PRAYER BOOK REVISION IN THE CHURCH IN WALES
SINCE 1920

HAVING ATTEMPTED some general account of the forces affecting the position of the 1662 Book in the Anglican Communion today, and having surveyed the movement towards the revision of it, we now turn to the Church in Wales.

I.   The Position of the 1662 Book after Disestablishment.

Until disestablishment and disendowment came into force on 31st March, 1920, the four ancient Welsh dioceses were part of the Province of Canterbury. As such, they were subject to that body of ecclesiastical law, compounded of ancient custom as recognised both by the Church and by the common law of the realm, of constitutions and canons made from the earliest centuries by duly accredited Councils of the Church, and of statutes enacted by Parliament, which then as now obtained in that Province. In the Welsh dioceses as well as others in the Province, the 1662 Book was binding not only because the Convocation of the Province had approved it, but also because it had statutory force as being a schedule annexed to the Act of Uniformity, 1662.

The Welsh Church Act, 1914, dissolved all ecclesiastical law "as law", that is to say, as part of the law of the Realm. Having done this, the Act provided that as from the date of disestablishment, the ecclesiastical law of the Church of England, subject to any modifications made by disestablishment or to be made afterwards by competent authority in the Church in Wales, should "be binding on the members for the time being of the Church in Wales as if they had mutually agreed to be so bound". The 1662 Book was of course included in these provisions ; it was to prevail in the Church in Wales no longer because of the statutory force of the Act of Uniformity, 1662, but because of the assent of the members of the Church in Wales which the Welsh Church Act assumed.

The continued authority of the 1662 Book in this Province, however, was not left to depend solely upon the provisions of the Welsh Church Act. Not only did the Constitution of the Church in Wales (ch. II, § 30) prescribe that the Governing Body at its creation should accept the 1662 Book with whatever variations were made necessary by Disestablishment : it also enacted (ch. VII, §61) that among the declarations to be made at ordination, institution to a benefice, and on being licensed as an assistant curate, there should be one promising to use "the form in the said Book prescribed, and none other, except so far as shall be ordered by lawful authority".

Taken together, these enactments made it abundantly clear that until "lawful authority" ordained otherwise, only the 1662 Book might legally be used in the Church in Wales. In 1945, the Provincial Court heard an appeal by the Vicar and Churchwardens of Landore against the refusal of a faculty by the Chancellor of the Diocese of Swansea and Brecon. The Court's judgment discussed fully the ground and nature of the obligation to use 1662 in this Province. After reviewing the provisions of the Welsh Church Act, 1914, and of the Constitution of the Church in Wales, the Court concluded that the contents of the Act of Uniformity 1662, together with the Book annexed to it, prevail in the Church in Wales not as still possessing the force of an Act of Parliament, "but by reason of the fact that the members of the Church in Wales have by contract assented to its terms as part of the ecclesiastical law of the Church in Wales". This judgment will long stand as an authoritative and detailed account of the position of 1662 in this Province.[28]

II. Developments between 1920 and 1950 ; The "Nation and Prayer Book" Commission.

Disestablishment made the Church in Wales an autonomous Province of the Anglican Communion, free to order its own affairs in any way not inconsistent with the teaching and discipline of the Catholic Church. So far as Prayer Book revision is concerned, this freedom is explicitly recognised in our Constitution, which says (Chapter II, §34) "The Governing Body shall have power to make alterations in . . . rites, ceremonies, and formularies . . . . by a Bill . . . backed and introduced in the Governing Body by a

(28) The enactments cited in this section are given in full in Appendix I. The relevant parts of the Provincial Court's judgment in the Landore case are printed as Appendix D of the "Nation and Prayer Book" Report, pp. 89-91. See also C. A. H. Green, *The Setting of the Constitution of the Church in Wales*, London 1937, pp. 95-99. The latest edition of the Constitution of the Church in Wales is that revised in 1956, and printed at Cardiff.

majority of the Bishops . . . ."[29]

It is important to note two points about this section. On the one hand, it preserves to the Bishops that initiative in the formulation of doctrine and the ordering of worship which has always been inherent in their office and has been recognised by the tradition of the Church. On the other hand, it recognises that in this Province the supreme legislative power resides in the Governing Body, representative as it is of the whole Church in Wales through the association of elected representatives of the clergy and laity with the Bishops in the ordering of her affairs. As we shall see, both these facts are vital for the right understanding of the Canon governing the issue of services for experimental use which the Governing Body adopted in September, 1956.

The pressure of more immediate problems arising from Disestablishment, and a deep attachment to 1662 in both its versions which still persists, made the Church in Wales cautious in approaching the matter of Prayer Book revision. In the period 1920-1947, however, a few steps were taken, and the Governing Body debated the desirability of revision on three occasions.

At Easter, 1924, the Governing Body promulgated a Canon allowing the use of the 1922 English Lectionary as an alternative to the Lectionary of 1871. In actual practice the position had been that the Lectionary most used in our parishes has been the Lectionary of 1922 as revised in 1928, the use of which is not legal here on a strict interpretation of the Canon. As will be explained later, the Governing Body took further action over the Lectionary in September, 1956.[30]

Two other positive measures were adopted during the period under review. First, in September, 1933, the Governing Body promulgated a Canon authorising the holding of Ordinations on the Saturdays in the Ember weeks. As the late Archbishop Green explained, the motives for the adoption of this Canon were partly a wish to return to the ancient custom of this country, and partly considerations of practical convenience and the wish to resolve the clash between Canon 31 of the 1603/4 Canons and the Preface to the Ordinal, the former of which confines Ordinations to the Sundays immediately following the Ember Weeks, while the latter

(29) See Appendix I for the full text of this and the following sections.

(30) See Appendix II for the full text of this Canon.

24

allows them, "on urgent occasion, upon some other Sunday or Holy Day".[31]

The other specific matter dealt with was one of much wider interest. In April, 1936, the Governing Body requested the Archbishop and Diocesan Bishops to make proposals, among other things, for a Calendar of Welsh Saints. The late Archbishop (Dr. John Morgan) drew up a Calendar which the Bench of Bishops approved. The outbreak of war prevented its presentation to the Governing Body till September, 1944. An amendment asking the Bench to reconsider it was heavily defeated, and the Report incorporating it was adopted. It will be observed that this Calendar possesses only the authority of its adoption by the Governing Body, and not that of a Canon duly promulgated after Bill procedure. It divides the Saints contained in it into two grades of importance. It confines itself strictly to the scope of a Calendar, and attempts nothing by way of liturgical provision beyond suggesting that when St. David's Day falls outside Lent, the Octave of that Festival should be observed throughout the Province; and that the Octaves of other Saints of the first rank should be observed in the dioceses or parishes of which they are the Patron Saints. The dates given to individual Saints have provoked a certain amount of learned disagreement; it is very doubtful whether a higher degree of chronological exactitude can be obtained in respect of men and women much of the history of whose age, like Creusa's ghost,

"Ter frustra comprensa manus effugit imago,
par levibus ventis volucrique simillima somno."[32]

We must now describe the attempts made to launch a full-scale revision during this period. The first was in September, 1922, when the following motion was proposed in the Governing Body:—
"That the Bishops be respectfully requested to consider and report on any changes and additions that may be desired in the Book of Common Prayer, including the Title Page of the Welsh edition of the Prayer Book, special prayers for various occasions, the appointment of a special Collect for St. David's Day, and any other changes made necessary by the present altered position of the Church in Wales". Its sponsors eventually withdrew this motion, and there matters rested till 1927. The debates over the English revised Book

(31) See Appendix II. *Cf.* C. A. H. Green, *op. cit.*, p. 106.

(32) Virgil, *Aeneid*, II, 793-4. The text of the Calendar is given in Appendix II.

25

were then in full career, and doubtless because of the speculation they were stirring in this Province, the Archbishop (Dr. A. G. Edwards), made the following statement on behalf of the Bishops to the Governing Body when it met at Easter in that year:— "We are of the opinion that, as the decisions of the Convocation of Canterbury, made since Disestablishment, and the measures of the National Assembly of the Church of England, have no authority nor force in the Province of Wales, it is now and will always be illegal to use any Book of Common Prayer other than that accepted by the Governing Body of the Church in Wales (Chapter II, Section 30) in any of the Churches of the Province of Wales until or except such Book of Common Prayer be revised or altered by the Governing Body under the Bill procedure as presented in Chapter II, Section 34, of the Constitution of the Church in Wales".

This statement did not deter members of the Governing Body from bringing before it, in September, 1927, a motion in these terms: —"That the Archbishop and Bishops of the Church in Wales be respectfully requested to appoint a Committee to consider and report on the adoption and translation of the Revised Prayer Book" (*i.e.*, the English Deposited Book). The Archbishop in reply said:— "The Archbishop and Bishops . . . . wish it to be understood that they will not take any action until, in their opinion, the proper moment has arrived". An attempt to move the previous question was rejected, and the original motion was carried by a large marjotiy. The Bench of Bishops, however, adhered to its attitude, and did not act on the motion.

Sixteen years were to pass before the question again came before the Governing Body. In September, 1943, it was moved:—"That the Governing Body of the Church in Wales make request to the Lord Archbishop that he in consultation with the other Bishops of the Province would appoint a Commission :—

(*a*) To consider such permissive deviations from the Book of Common Prayer (as it is now in use in the Province) whether by way of alteration or of addition, as may be thought desirable.

(*b*) To report from time to time to the Lord Archbishop."

After a full debate, the motion was heavily defeated, partly or largely, it appears, after a powerful speech by the late Lord Atkin in which he emphasised the legal ties binding the Province to 1662, and stressed the unwisdom of dividing nation and Church in a time of war.

The first twenty-three years after Disestablishment, therefore, saw nothing done towards a large-scale revision of 1662. In 1922, the upheaval of Disestablishment was too recent. In 1927, the Governing Body as a whole were favourable to the possibility of taking over the 1928 Book in this Province; the Bishops however, wisely as we must now think, held their hand. In 1943, the circumstances of the time and the weight of the opposition produced a decisive refusal to go forward. A few years later, the scene had altered. The period immediately following the end of hostilities saw in the Church in Wales marked interest in and widespread discussion of her place in the nation's life. One of the results of this was that the Governing Body adopted a motion in September, 1946, which led the Bench of Bishops, in April, 1947, to appoint the Commission generally known as the "Nation and Prayer Book" Commission. To quote the terms of the motion which secured its appointment, this body was asked to consider "what reforms might be made to put the Church in a better position to take a larger part in the life of the nation, and in particular, as preparation for a possible revision of the Book of Common Prayer, to report upon :

(1) The present position in Canon Law as to the Prayer Book and Lectionary.

(2) The various revisions of the Prayer Book which have been undertaken in other Provinces of the Church".

The Commission presented its Report to the Governing Body in September, 1949.[33] Its findings and recommendations on Prayer Book revision are to be found in Part III., pp. 58-79, and the two appendices contained in pp. 89-98; and they may be summarised thus.

(1) The Commission felt its first duty to be the payment of due tribute to the 1662 Book as magnificently expressing the liturgical conception of Christian worship, and as enshrining those standards of doctrine and worship accepted by the Anglican Communion as a whole. However good a case there is for revision, no revision can be effective unless it is coupled with an intensified effort to teach our people the principles of liturgical worship, and to foster in them a

(33) See Note 10 above.

27

greater appreciation of the merits of our existing Book.

It may be fairly claimed that all experience since has brought out the importance of the point just recalled. Not only has the work of revision made clearer to those immediately involved the magnitude of the achievement which 1662 represents; it has also become plain that the revision of it cannot hope to be understood or accepted unless the issue of revised services for experimental use is accompanied by a sustained effort to explain to Churchpeople in general the principles upon which revision is undertaken, and the problems which it seeks to meet.

(2) The Commission next examined the case for revising 1662 in this Province. This part of its investigations came under two heads:—

(*a*) In accordance with its terms of reference, the Commission examined the present position of the Prayer Book and Lectionary in Canon Law, and discussed certain legal and constitutional anomalies in which our retention of 1662 involves us. It was pointed out, for example, that the words "according to the use of the Church of England" on the title page, as well as other parts of 1662, are a direct denial of the self-governing position of this Province. The Report also discussed the legal difficulties arising from those sections of the Act of 1563 and the Act of Uniformity, 1662, which govern the translation of the Prayer Book into Welsh : this part of the Report led to the first recommendation given below. The Lectionary received similar examination. Besides pointing out the anomaly involved in permitting by Canon the use of the 1922 Lectionary when in fact the majority of churches used the amended version of that Lectionary adopted in 1928, the Report raised a further issue. How far is the Canon in question consistent with independent action in any one diocese of the Province permitting the use of another Lectionary, the Bishop concerned having taken his stand on the directions of the 1662 Book entitled "The Order how the Rest of the Holy Scripture is to be read"?

(*b*) The Commission next discussed the pastoral considerations favouring revision of 1662 in the Church in Wales. After appealing to the principles laid down by resolution 27 of the

1909 Lambeth Conference,[34] the Commission stated its own findings under these heads :—

(i) **Rubrics.** There is need for the excision of obsolete rubrics; for the provision of new ones to regularise a number of practices which have become customary but of whose strict legality there is doubt; and for the expansion of certain rubrics, particularly the "Ornaments Rubric" before Morning Prayer, so as to make clear what they allow or do not allow.

(ii) **The Holy Communion.** There is required (1) a fuller provision of Propers for the lesser Saints' Days, for occasions such as Patronal and Dedication Festivals, Missions, and Retreats, and for the great family occasions of marriage and death. A greater number of Proper Prefaces should also be supplied;

(2) the regulation of such variations from the Order of 1662 as are of long standing in the liturgical tradition of Christendom, and do not represent a departure from the doctrinal standards of 1662.

(iii) **Morning and Evening Prayer.** (1) So that full justice may be done to both the great ministries of the Gospel, it may well be desirable to allow a shortened form of Mattins which could be followed by the Holy Communion, without making the whole service overlong.

(2) There is a case for an alternative ending to the Litany suitable for times of peace.

(3) There is a need to provide for an ordered and shortened list of Psalms to be sung on Sundays, to combat the individualism now common in this matter.

(4) It is widely felt that the present Sunday Lessons are not in some instances those best calculated to edify.

(34) "In any revision of the Book of Common Prayer which may hereafter be undertaken by competent authority the following principles should be held in view : (a) The adaptation of rubrics in a large number of cases to present customs as generally accepted ; (b) The omission of parts of the services to obviate repetition or redundancy; (c) The framing of additions to the present services in the way of enrichment; (d) The fuller provision of alternatives in our forms of public worship; (e) The provision for greater elasticity in public worship; (f) the change of words obscure or commonly misunderstood; (g) The revision of the Calendar and Tables prefixed to the Book of Common Prayer."

(5) It is desirable to find some method of impressing upon the clergy their obligation to recite Mattins and Evensong daily. There are wide variations of practice in the Province at present in this respect. The renewed emphasis upon this obligation might be coupled with encouragement of the devout laity who can do so to join in the Daily Office.

(iv) **The Occasional Offices.** In varying degrees, these Offices "afford scope for a revision whose aim would be two-fold, (I) to enhance their proper importance as sacramental rites or as a means of seeking the Divine Blessing upon major turning-points of human life, (2) to increase their effectiveness as a means of commending the Gospel at those turning points".[35] Judged by these standards and in the light of modern parish life, all the existing Offices require attention. The Baptismal services suffer from obscurities of language and Biblical reference, and from the private and hurried fashion in which Baptism is often administered. The Marriage service also contains unhelpful archaisms. The Order for the Visitation and Communion of the Sick neither gives satisfactorily the best Christian teaching on health and sickness, nor does it prove easy to use, particularly the Communion, in the populous parish of today. The Burial Office needs additional Psalms and Lessons, and commendatory prayer as well as prayers for the comforting of the bereaved and the strengthening of their faith.

(v) **The Occasional Prayers and Thanksgivings.** There is a clear need for a fuller provision by authority. But the prayers added must be good, and restraint must be exercised over their number.

(vi) **Additional Services.** There are needed : (1) Services for use on occasions when most of those present are not regular worshippers, and designed to help the un-instructed along the path of liturgical worship.

(2) Children's Services.[36]

(35) Report, p. 73.

(36) Since the date of the Report, the Children's Council of the Church in Wales has produced a book of these Services which the Bishops have approved, and which is widely appreciated and used.

(3) Services for Youth Fellowships.

(4) Family Prayers.

(vii) **The Welsh Version of the Prayer Book.** The Report discussed this matter under two heads, language and orthography, and the Prayer Book and the existing social structure of Wales. The main conclusions to which the Commission came have already been outlined in the first part of this study and there is no need to repeat them here.[37]

(3) In the light of these facts, the Commission felt justified in concluding that the time was ripe for the Church in Wales to undertake a systematic revision of 1662. In the third section of Part III, the Report gave the Commission's conclusions arising from its study of revision in other Provinces. It was thought that the best course, followed in many Provinces, was to revise in stages with time for experiment, and to make revision the work of the whole body of the Church. The fruits of revision elsewhere should be borne in mind and closely studied throughout.

Three specific recommendations arose from Part III of the "Nation and Prayer Book" Report. The first aimed at clearing up the legal difficulties attaching to the translation of the Prayer Book into Welsh, and read as follows:—"That the Governing Body adopt a resolution in the following terms:—'It is hereby declared that those provisions of the Welsh Act, 1563, and of Section 27 of the Act of Uniformity 1662, relating to the translation of the Book of Common Prayer into the Welsh language, shall in future have no effect in the Province of Wales and that the Governing Body shall have power to make such arrangements as it sees fit for the publication of a Welsh version of the Book of Common Prayer'."

The second recommendation attempted to secure the adoption of general principles governing the work of revision, and ran thus:— "That the Governing Body adopt a resolution in the following terms:—'The Governing Body considers it desirable that the following general principles should govern any measure of Prayer Book revision undertaken in this Province, namely:—

(37) See pp. 3, 5, above.

(*a*) A beginning should be made with such changes in the existing Prayer Book as are required by pastoral and practical considerations.

(*b*) No attempt should be made at any large scale revision at any one time, rather, such changes as may be desirable and generally acceptable should be authorised in stages'."

The third recommendation dealt with the machinery for revision. Its terms were : "That the Governing Body request His Grace the Archbishop to appoint a Commission called the 'Standing Liturgical Commission', whose duty it shall be to submit from time to time recommendations to the Bench of Bishops concerning such amendments as may be necessary or desirable in the Church's law of worship, and that the Archibishop be respectfully requested to ensure that the composition of the Commission adequately reflects different points of view within the Church, in particular through the inclusion among its members of:—

(*a*) Liturgical scholars and theologians.

(*b*) Persons of trained literary capacity.

(*c*) Persons of wide pastoral, administrative and practical experience."

All these recommendations were debated at the meeting of the Governing Body on 13th April, 1950. The first was adopted after deleting the words " of section 27". The Commission agreed to withdraw the second after it had been represented that if adopted, it might tie unduly the hands of the Bishops and others immediately associated with them in the work of revision. The third recommendation met with two proposed amendments. The second of these sought to delete the words after "His Grace the Archbishop" and to substitute the words "to appoint Assessors whose duty it shall be:—

(*a*) to study liturgical problems;

(*b*) to submit from time to time amendments to the Bench of Bishops concerning the Church's law of worship".

Both amendments were defeated, and the original motion was carried *nemine contradicente*. So it was that the Church in Wales, in the thirtieth year after disestablishment, decided to take in hand a general revision of 1662.

III. Since 1951 : Status and Procedure of the Standing Liturgical Commission : The Issue of Revised Services for Experimental Use.

The Standing Liturgical Commission of the Church in Wales was appointed in January, 1951. It held its first meeting at Llandrindod on 28th March, 1951. Its first Chairman was the Very Reverend W. G. H. Simon, then Dean, now Bishop of Llandaff. He resigned on his election as Bishop of Swansea and Brecon, and was succeeded in January, 1954, as Chairman by his successor in the Deanery of Llandaff, the Very Reverend Eryl S. Thomas. The first Secretary of the Commission was the Reverend O. G. Rees, at the time of his appointment Sub-Warden, and now Warden, of St. Michael's College, Llandaff. Mr. Rees resigned the Secretaryship in January, 1956, on his preferment to the benefice of Aberdare. The Commission's first major act was to circulate to all incumbents a Questionnaire covering in detail the Holy Communion, Morning and Evening Prayer and the Litany, and the Occasional Offices. The Questionnaire also contained a short general section, and the letter accompanying it invited incumbents to write to the Commission stating what parts of 1662 in their view most urgently needed revision, and their reasons for saying so. The body of information collected through the Questionnaire cleared the ground, and the memoranda compiled from it by the then Secretary will long continue to be of the utmost value for the Commission's work.

It is important to make clear at the outset what the status of this Commission is, and the more so in that experience has revealed the existence of much misunderstanding about its function and powers. To recall its terms of reference as set out in the Governing Body resolution of April 1950, it is a body appointed by the Archbishop, and its duty is "to submit from time to time recommendations to the Bench of Bishops concerning such amendments as may be necessary or desirable in the Church's law of worship". Two points emerge from these instructions.

First, the Commission is charged to report its findings neither to the Church in Wales at large nor to the Governing Body, but to the Bench of Bishops. It will readily be understood that this fact imposes upon the Commission a most binding degree of secrecy concerning the discussions at its meetings.

Second, the Commission is not a body possessing plenary

powers in the matter of Prayer Book revision. It is a body set up to help and advise the Bench of Bishops. By the ancient law of the Church, expressly recognised in Chapter 2 of our Constitution, it is the Bishops who possess the initiative and final responsibility in bringing forward any measures affecting doctrine, worship, and ceremonial. When we see, as we shall often see in the future, revised services assented to by the Governing Body and authorised for use in the dioceses, one thing ought to be clearly understood, and that is this. Whatever part the Liturgical Commission has played in drawing up a particular service, the Bishops are in no way bound by its recommendations; the responsibility for the final form which a service takes, and for bringing it before the Governing Body, is theirs alone. Another point to be noted is this. From time to time, suggestions and criticisms, and requests for specific action on one liturgical matter or another, are sent to the Commission. The Commission is glad, indeed anxious, to receive and consider any suggestions bearing upon its task. But it cannot of its own power undertake liturgical projects at the request of individuals or committees or groups, however desirable this or that suggested reform may seem to it to be. The Commission can act only upon directions from the Bench of Bishops speaking in the name of the Province as a whole.

As has been said, the Commission is obliged to secrecy about the discussions at its meetings. That does not mean, however, that our faithful churchpeople and others interested should not have some idea of the methods by which it does the work entrusted to it. At present it is a body of twenty-three persons, of whom eighteen are clergymen, and five laymen.[38]   Full meetings are held three or four times a year, generally at Llandaff. In between full meetings, four sub-committees are at work, namely Occasional Offices, Lectionary and Psalter, Drafting, and Welsh Translation. It is the function of the first two of these sub-committees to lay preliminary drafts of proposals for revision before their parent body. Each of these drafts receives three readings, the first general, the others involving a very close scrutiny of details. The third reading ended, the draft goes to the Drafting sub-committee, and is given a final polishing in point of language, style, and punctuation. The draft then goes to the Bishops without further reference to the Commission. During the later stages of the debates within the Commis-

(38) See Appendix III for the list of members.

34

sion, the Welsh Translation sub-committee will also have been at work, and will have submitted preliminary drafts of the Welsh version.

When the draft reaches the Bench of Bishops, it is subjected to another scrutiny of the most minute sort. In one way or another, the Bench keeps in touch with the Commission at this stage, and there is due exchange of views. When the Bishops have finally settled the English text, the Welsh Translation sub-committee once more comes into play, and the two versions are printed together and submitted to the Governing Body.

It has already been explained that the Bishops of the Church in Wales possess by ancient right and positive enactment the initiative in proposing measures which concern doctrine, discipline, worship and ceremonial. But we have also noted that the possession and exercise of that initiative must take account of the fact that the supreme legislative power in the Church in Wales does not reside in the Bishops alone, but in the Governing Body, which comprises representatives of the inferior clergy and the laity as well as the Bench of Bishops. When the first proposals for revision were nearing finality, it became needful to devise a procedure authorising their use which would respect the rights of Governing Body and Bishops alike. This was done by a Canon adopted by the Governing Body in September, 1956, and entitled "Experimental Use of Proposed Revisions of the Book of Common Prayer, provisionally approved by the Bench of Bishops". The full text of this Canon is given in Appendix II, but it will be convenient to quote here the operative part of it:—

. . . . "WHEREAS in the opinion of the Bench of Bishops it may be desirable that before a Bill for the revision of a part or parts of the Book of Common Prayer is submitted to the Governing Body the proposed revision should be used experimentally in the parishes for a limited period.

BE IT HEREBY ENACTED THAT:—

(1) A diocesan bishop shall have power to authorise for experimental use in the churches within his diocese any proposed revision of a part or parts of the Book of Common Prayer which have been provisionally approved by the Bench of Bishops, provided that the said authorisation shall be for a limited period not exceeding ten years and provided that the Governing Body shall

have assented to the experimental use of the proposed revision without alteration.

(2) A bishop shall not take action under Clause 1 hereof until after the next meeting of the Governing Body following the circulation to the members of the Governing Body of printed copies of the proposed revision."

Let us examine the salient features of this legislation. There is to be no attempt to secure the adoption of a complete revised Prayer Book at one stroke. Revision is to proceed piecemeal. At each stage, the results of it are to be subjected to a preliminary period of experimental use in the parishes. The regulations governing this process carefully safeguard the rights both of the Governing Body and of the Bishops. Not only does the Governing Body retain its power of final decision, by the Bill procedure laid down in the Constitution, whether a revised service is or is not to become part of the law of worship of the Church in Wales : it also has the absolute power at the beginning to give or withhold assent to the experimental use of a revised service. The rights of the Bishops are safeguarded not only because no revised service can be submitted to the Governing Body unless the Bench as a whole has approved of it, but also because the Governing Body's assent still leaves individual bishops free to authorise or forbid the experimental use of a revised service in their dioceses.

Such is the procedure for Prayer Book revision which the Church in Wales has decided to adopt. The obvious criticism of it is that it is cumbersome and involves the passing of many years before finality is reached. One is tempted to murmur an *ars longa, vita brevis* over it : and to mention one feature of it in particular, it is legitimate to question whether to have allowed the Bishops to sanction by the inherent power of their office the experimental use of revised services, as was originally intended, really constituted an infringement of the Governing Body's rights as the supreme legislative organ of the Church in Wales. The form finally taken by the 1956 Canon does not exclude the possibility that an emotional and ill-informed or ill-managed debate when a revised service is submitted for the Governing Body's assent might mean prejudicing that service's chance of a fair trial from the start. Be that as it may, our procedure as a whole can lay claim to solid merits; what these merits are can be conveniently shown by discussing the fate of the 1928 English Book.

The 1928 Book has been severely criticised on the ground that much of its language is too humanist. Further, some of its specific proposals, particularly those relating to the Holy Communion service and to Reservation, provoked intense controversy. Nevertheless vast labours had gone to the making of it, and its revision of rubrics, the changes and additions made in the Occasional Offices, its increased provision of Propers, and other new matter, all represented a distinct advance.

Why did all this end in the Book's rejection? Apart from the deep disagreement on central issues of doctrine which dogged its career, one may at this distance of time single out two weaknesses.

First, in the compilation of the Book, help was indeed sought from experts as need required. From 1912 to 1918, the work was assisted by an "Advisory Committee on Liturgical Questions" representative of both Provinces. This Committee was hampered by its terms of reference, and some of its most valuable proposals were rejected, nevertheless, several important features of 1928 can be traced to its work. After 1918, the Bishops worked more and more in isolation. At no stage of the proceedings from 1906 onwards were they assisted by any body at all corresponding to the Standing Liturgical Commission here, set up by the Archbishop with adequate terms of reference at the request of the Governing Body, representative of the clergy and laity of the Province as a whole, and meeting regularly and working in accordance with a definite plan. Such being the procedure, it was inevitable that the 1928 Book should be suspected as issuing from the brains of the Bishops alone, and as being an attempt on their part to end quickly the liturgical chaos which was troubling them. These suspicions had much to do with the Book's ultimate failure.

But another major weakness undermined the Book. The attempt was made to give the whole of it lawful authority at one blow. Its proposals were indeed exhaustively debated in the Convocations and the Church Assembly. But these debates for the most part were not widely heeded, and when they were it was only when matters of controversy were to the fore. There was no period of prolonged experiment during which the general body of the clergy and the laity in the parishes could have a fair chance to try out the revised services and learn the reasons for changes. This too made for rejection, and rejection in a heated and prejudiced atmosphere.[39]

Coming late into the field, the Church in Wales has had time to reflect both on the misfortunes of her neighbouring Provinces and on the experience of Prayer Book revision gained in other parts of the Anglican Communion. We have sought to make the work a work of the whole Church by enlisting the services of men representing all sections of her members, and by seeing to it that through the experimental period, every parish should contribute towards the final decision. A period of experiment has been the general rule in other Provinces except the English ones. We in Wales have been the gainers. We have learned the wisdom of going one step at a time. And we can profit to the full from the scholarly researches which this age of liturgical experiment is stimulating. The work, let it be repeated, has begun here as a work of the whole Church. If it is to have an happy ending, it must continue on those lines. It is the duty of all faithful members of the Church in Wales to give the revised services a fair trial, to discuss and criticise them with understanding, and to make their views known to those immediately responsible for the revision.

(39) For the later stages in the history of the 1928 Book, see G. K. A. Bell, *Randall Davidson*, vol. II, Ch. 82, pp. 1325-1360. A most important source of information is R. C. D. Jasper, *Walter Howard Frere. His Correspondence on Liturgical Revision and Construction;* Alcuin Club Collections No. 39, London, 1954; for the "Advisory Committee on Liturgical Questions" see ch. 2, pp. 26-55, and particularly pp. 53-55. A most useful study of the 1928 Book's proposals is W. K. L. Clarke, *The Prayer Book of* 1928 *Reconsidered*, London, 1943.

C

PROPOSALS FOR REVISION SO FAR APPROVED FOR EXPERIMENTAL USE IN THE CHURCH IN WALES

THOUGH it is not possible to discuss the matter in detail, it may be said that in the seven years during which it has been at work, the industry of its Occasional Offices and Lectionary and Psalter sub-committees has already enabled the Standing Liturgical Commission to cover a great deal of the ground before it. So far, the Governing Body has given assent to the experimental use of two pieces of revision. These are a revised Lectionary and Table of Proper Psalms for Sundays and certain other days, presented to the Governing Body in September, 1956: and the revised services of Baptism and Confirmation, presented to the Governing Body at Easter, 1957. This concluding section attempts some account of both.

I. The Revised Lectionary and Table of Proper Psalms for Sundays and certain other Days.

Until September, 1956, the only Tables of Lessons for Sundays and weekdays which could be used in the Church in Wales were the Lectionary of 1871 as printed in the Book of Common Prayer, or the Lectionary of 1922 adopted as an alternative to the 1871 Lectionary by the Governing Body Canon of 1924.[40] We also adhered to the provision for reciting the Psalter made in the Book of Common Prayer, namely, its monthly recitation in sixty portions subject to the Table of Proper Psalms to be used on certain days contained in that Book.

In October, 1955, the English Convocations authorised a new Lectionary for use in the Church of England as from Advent, 1956. Thenceforward, the 1871 and 1922 Lectionaries would cease to be used or published in England. These changes confronted the Church in Wales with a serious difficulty. For the Lectionaries hitherto legal in the Church in Wales would not now be readily available. Furthermore, although the Standing Liturgical Commission had done a good deal of work on the Lectionary, the work had not reached a stage when a complete and separate Church in Wales Lectionary could be published and put into use. Finality had, however, been reached in the Commission as regards the

(40) See p. 24 above.

Lessons and Proper Psalms for Sundays and certain other days. It was felt that the best solution of the problem was to secure the experimental use of a Lectionary which would follow the 1955 Lectionary in the matter of week day lessons, but would incorporate, so far as Sundays and certain other days were concerned, the proposals of the Commission regarding Lessons and Proper Psalms as considered and amended by the Bench of Bishops. S.P.C.K. readily agreed to publish what was in effect a Welsh edition of the 1955 Lectionary, and the proposed arrangement, as has been said, received the Governing Body's assent in September, 1956. This assent in no way prevents the continued use, if desired, of the 1871 or 1922 Lectionaries on Sundays and weekdays.

On what plan have the experimental Lectionary and Table of Psalms been drawn up? First, the Lectionary. It gives two Tables, A and B, to be used in alternate years. Except on Palm Sunday morning, no alternative Lessons are given. The general aim has been that shorter Lessons should be read in the morning, and that so far as possible no morning Lesson should exceed twenty verses. From Advent to Trinity Sunday, the Lessons are mostly an anthology, but the reading of Isaiah in Advent, and of Genesis and Hebrews in Lent, preserves a due amount of sequence during those seasons; the same regard for custom has applied to the Great Festivals. From the first Sunday after Trinity to the Sunday next before Advent, both Tables follow a sequence, that at Mattins being independent from that at Evensong. In Table A, there are read at Mattins lessons from the Wisdom literature, and from Hosea, Amos and Micah; the New Testament readings at Mattins are from St. Mark, the Pastoral Epistles, and Revelation. At Evensong in Table A, the Old Testament readings are from Numbers, the historical Books, Jeremiah and Ezekiel, and 1 and 2 Maccabees; the New Testament readings are from Acts, Romans, and St. John. In Table B, at Mattins the Old Testament readings for the greater part are from the same books as are drawn upon for Evensong in Table A; the New Testament readings are from St. Luke and the Pauline Epistles. At Evensong in Table B, the Old Testament readings come from much the same books as those used for Mattins in Table A, but there is a wider selection from the Minor Prophets; the New Testament readings are from St. Matthew, the Pastoral Epistles not used at Mattins in Table A, and from Revelation. Points of detail to be noted are the increased use of the Apocrypha, the provision that the Lessons for Epiphany V and VI are to serve also on Trinity XXV and XXVI, and the attempt where possible to bring together Old Testament prophecies, and incidents and passages of the New Testament referring to them. Those responsible would be the first to admit that this scheme does not cover all the passages which well deserve a place; the answer, it may be, is by providing a third Table.

The Table of Psalms aims at covering as much of the Psalter as possible. For various reasons which make their congregational use difficult in this age, eight Psalms are omitted altogether (14, 35, 58, 64, 70, 79, 83, 109): and Psalm 88 is used on Good Friday only. It has been attempted to keep within reasonable length each portion of the Psalter provided, the longer Psalms coming mostly at Evensong. In the Psalms chosen, no verses are omitted : and it is suggested that where it is difficult to sing a complete portion, some of it, if not all of it, might be said. Proper Psalms have been provided for the Feast of the Circumcision and its Eve when either falls on a Sunday. Where there are more than twenty-five Sundays after Trinity, the Psalms for the last two Sundays after the Epiphany are to be used. The Table remains the same year after year, and among other things the observance of it means that most of the best Psalms come twice in the year, alternating between Mattins and Evensong. As other problems concerning the Lectionary and Psalter still await consideration, the Table is issued on the understanding that it should be subject to revision at a later date in the light of decisions made on those problems.[41]

II. The Revised Services of Baptism and Confirmation.

This group of services, the first group of which the experimental use has received assent from the Governing Body and authorisation from the diocesan Bishops, comprises Public Baptism of Infants, Private Baptism of Infants and Reception into the Congregation, Adult Baptism, and Confirmation. The Llan and Welsh Church Press has published the revised services in various forms, all readily available from the Church in Wales Provincial Council for Education, Llandaff House, Penarth; the booklet containing all the services, and giving the English and Welsh texts on parallel pages

(41) Most of the matter contained in this section is based upon the printed Reports of the Standing Liturgical Commission presented to the Governing Body in September, 1956, together with the printed statement by the Bench of Bishops presented in conjunction with these Reports.

41

(price 1/6), affords the most convenient means of studying them.[42]

To begin with, some account must be given of the historical and doctrinal considerations borne in mind in the revision of these services. These considerations are two-fold :

(1) As is well known, the services here in question are closely linked together in that from the earliest times they have been the rites through which persons have been initiated into membership of the Catholic Church. The Eastern Church continues to witness to their inter-relation in the clearest way by its practice of administering Baptism, Confirmation, and Communion in a single service, and this to infants as well as adults. In the West, matters developed differently. At least from the 3rd century A.D. it had become the common practice to baptize infants, departing from earlier custom by which membership of the Church was generally given to adults only, after a course of instruction and by means of a rite which included Confirmation as well as Baptism. Caused by the rapid growth of the Church in the first place, this development in itself tended to separate Confirmation from Baptism, and the process was further accentuated by the growth of large territorial dioceses whose towns and villages could only rarely be visited by their Bishop, who remained the minister of Confirmation in the West as he did not in the East. Thus arose the familiar situation by which Baptism and Confirmation, originally linked together in one rite of Christian initiation, have become separated from each other so far as their administration is concerned.

Down the centuries, the development just outlined has provided the theologians of Western Christendom with abundant material for debate. How exactly are Baptism and Confirmation related? Does God the Holy Spirit operate in both or only one of these rites? How are the effects of His operation to be defined? These and allied questions have never been without their investigators and are still being pursued vigorously in modern Anglicanism. According to one school of thought, at Baptism the Holy Spirit is given in all His fullness, and to that extent Confirmation is less important.

(42) The present Archbishop of Wales, Dr. A. E. Morris, has discussed the revised services in an article in the *Church Times* of January 31, 1958, p. 11. In *Province* Autumn, 1957, pp. 90-94, Christmas, 1957, pp. 125-130, and Easter 1958, pp. 25-32. F. W. G. Griffiths has published the first three parts of an extended study of the services. The present writer would like to express his indebtedness to both these accounts.

Others maintain on the contrary that Confirmation bestows so abundant a gift of the Holy Spirit that Baptism not followed by Confirmation is almost a maimed rite. A recent authoritative account of these matters concludes with the words : "The complexity of the evidence is such as to suggest that a final solution will not be reached by an appeal to history".[43]

The Welsh revisers would agree with that conclusion. While the debates on these crucial questions are still going on vigorously, it seemed unwise to produce services whose language might appear to tie the Church in Wales down to this or that view of them. It has not been forgotten, either, that there *are* matters of doctrine which it is the genius of Anglicanism not to define too rigidly. The debates however do not affect, indeed they have served to emphasise even more clearly, the link between Baptism and Confirmation as component parts of the Christian initiation rites : and the revised services bear witness to that fact. For example, the second rubric prefacing Public Baptism of Infants, having enjoined upon parents their duty to bring their children to Baptism, goes on to say ". . . . it is their duty to see that their children are instructed in the Catechism and brought to the Bishop to be confirmed, that so they may be admitted to the Holy Communion". Again, the Priest's address at the conclusion of Infant and Adult Baptism makes it perfectly clear that Confirmation, with the privilege of admission to the Holy Communion which it bestows, is the normal and necessary complement to what is done at the Font. The link between the two rites is further brought out in the rubric in the Adult Baptism service which orders the omission of its concluding parts if Confirmation follows immediately, and by the rubric in the Confirmation service ordering that when the only candidates present are those whose Confirmation follows immediately upon their Baptism, the service shall begin at "Our help is in the Name of the Lord".

(2) Not only the doctrine of the Holy Spirit, but also that of Sin and Grace, is deeply involved in any consideration of Baptism

(43) *The Oxford Dictionary of the Christian Church*, article s.n. "Confirmation". This article, together with those on Baptism and Infant Baptism ,is to be commended for its concise and lucid accounts of the complicated questions involved. G. W. H. Lampe, *The Seal of the Spirit* (London, 1951), and L. S. Thornton, *Confirmation : Its place in the Baptismal Mystery* (London, 1954), are outstanding among recent Anglican studies of this subject.

and Confirmation; and here, the influence of St. Augustine is paramount in the West. In his Bampton Lectures on *The Ideas of the Fall and of Original Sin*, the late N. P. Williams finely compared Augustine to " . . . . a Colossus upon a mountain crest, marking the watershed between the ancient and the modern worlds, and casting its shadow far along the road . . . ."[44] Through his teaching on Original Sin and its effects, he certainly cast his shadow on the Anglican Baptismal rite : and some outline of his views must now be given.

St. Augustine's account of human nature is based upon the opening chapters of Genesis together with other Biblical texts, of which Psalm 51[5], St. John 3[5], and Romans 5[12] are the chief. His interpretation of Genesis 1-3 is literal to the point of making the serpent a real serpent, endowed by Satan with powers of speech so that he might become a more efficient instrument for the temptation of Eve. The sombre teaching which results is as follows.

In Paradise, Adam was by God's free gift a glorious being, immortal and omniscient. So long as it was maintained, the perfect balance between the various elements of his nature enabled him to avoid sin. But wittingly and consciously, he sinned. To what was his sin due? It was due, Augustine maintained, to "concupiscence". In its broad sense as used by Augustine, this word means, as Dr. Williams put it, "the tendency which impels man to turn from the supreme and immutable good, which is God, in order to find his satisfaction and comfort in that which is mutable and less than God, that is in creatures".[45] But in this instance Augustine limited its meaning to sexual lust. In the state of glory and bliss which God had bestowed upon him in Paradise, Adam could have begotten children in a purely rational manner. He fell, however, in large part because he had begun to burn with lust towards his wife, which made him the more ready to condone her surrender to the serpent and his blandishments.

The fall of Adam was not the fall of an isolated individual. It was the fall of one who contained in his loins the whole human race to the latest generation. Augustine was confirmed in this view because the Latin text of the Scriptures then current in Africa read, in Romans 5[12], *in quo*, which Augustine interpreted as "in Adam".

(44) London, 1927, p. 170. Lectures 5 and 6, pp. 317-446, treat fully of Augustine's teaching on human nature, sin, and grace, and its later developments.

(45) *Op. cit.* p. 365.

On the strength of this interpretation, he argued that Adam's fall infected not only himself, but all posterity as well, because posterity was contained in him when he sinned. This universal taint of human nature is transmitted from one generation to another in the course of the act of begetting children, and we call it *peccatum originale*, original or birth sin.

This calamity makes the position of mankind perilous indeed. In its natural state, all humanity is a mass of wickedness, doomed to Hell fire. Out of the mass, in His infinite wisdom and foreknowledge, God calls some to the waters of Baptism. Both the damned and the elect bear the guilt of original sin. Not only did all men fall in Adam, but inescapably and in their own persons they share with him the responsibility for the first act of disobedience towards God. In Baptism, we are indeed absolved from the guilt of original sin, but the permanent flaw inflicted by original sin upon our natures remains, and, undisciplined by the Divine grace, acts as a perpetual stimulus to sinful acts. Human nature has not indeed been utterly depraved by the Fall. It has nevertheless suffered so terrible a wound that man can do no good act without God's direct help leading him to do it and sustaining him in the doing of it : and without the gift of "final perseverance", which it is entirely within God's power to grant or withhold and which no efforts of ours can secure, no man may be saved.

The great Reformers, and Luther and Calvin above all, were more than willing disciples of Augustine on this point. The exaggerated features in his account of man's nature they exaggerated still further. They underlined his identification of "concupiscence" with sexual desire. He had not gone further, far as he *had* gone, than to point a wound in human nature which, deep as it was, still left in man some traces of goodness. The Reformers insisted on the total or almost total depravation of human kind. Such ravages has sin worked on man's nature that the image of God stamped upon it has been well-nigh obliterated, and man is utterly helpless to co-operate with God in repairing it. This advance in pessimism had as its natural corollary a more extreme insistence on the predestinarian elements in St. Augustine's teaching. In its Baptismal rites and elsewhere, these developments left their mark on the 1662 Book. Phrases such as "all men are conceived and born in sin", or "delivered from thy wrath", and other phrases implying a degree of original guilt, all flow from a thorough-going Augustinianism not consistent with the balanced teaching of the Church. Throughout the new Baptismal services, care has been taken to omit or modify expressions which either represent the act of procreation as inherently sinful, or countenance belief in the total depravation of human nature, or display God as an arbitrary and wrathful tyrant rather than the loving Father who wills all men to be saved and to come to the knowledge of the truth.

But whatever the exaggerations of St. Augustine and his disciples on the nature and destiny of man, the painful experience of humanity down the centuries bears clear testimony, as does the express message of the Bible, to the existence of a radical flaw in human nature which man's unassisted efforts can neither remove nor repair. In correcting false emphases produced by Augustinianism, have the revised services denied the being and depth of that flaw, and minimised the truth contained in the doctrines of the Fall and of Original Sin? It is a fair claim that the revised services have not erred in this respect. To quote phrases found in the exhortation near the beginning of the new service of Adult Baptism, there is "the sin which doth defile our human nature", and evil in us from whose dominion God wishes us to be delivered, antecedent to and distinct from the particular sins a man commits. The way to Christ cannot be opened at all, and entrance into His Kingdom cannot be won at all, unless the Divine grace takes the initiative and effects in us in our Baptism that profound and wonderful change which the Catechism calls "a death into sin, and a new birth unto righteousness". The new Baptismal services prefer indeed to speak of being "born again", or of "new birth", rather than of being "regenerate", as 1662 does. But the change of language implies no denial of the age-long doctrine of Baptismal Regeneration: nor is any countenance given to the idea that Baptism is a merely symbolic ceremony, and not an act in which, by the power of His Holy Spirit, God affects a real transformation and cleansing of natures hitherto lying under the tyranny of sin and evil and unable to receive the light of Christ.

Before we leave this discussion of Augustinianism and its effects on the Christian doctrine of human nature, sin and grace, together with its influence on the language of the 1662 Baptismal services, it will be convenient to note one important change in the revised Order of Confirmation. From very ancient times, before the candidates are confirmed the Bishop has said over them the Prayer which in 1662, faithfully following the original Latin, begins with these words:—"Almighty and everliving God, who hast vouchsafed to regenerate these thy servants by Water and the Holy Ghost, and hast given unto them forgiveness of all their sins". As it stands, the latter part of this formula raises a serious difficulty. For when first composed, the Prayer had in mind baptised adults, Adult Baptism being then the normal practice. But by now, Baptism in infancy has long been the normal custom. However the theologians explain the 1662 form of words, it remains unsatisfactory that babes who have committed no actual sins should be represented as having received in their Baptism forgiveness of all their sins. In the Additional note G and elsewhere in his Bampton Lectures, Dr. N. P. Williams brought out this point and other related problems with much learning and force. Other Anglican revisions have not faced the issue, but the Welsh revised Order has attempted to solve the contradiction by substituting for the words quoted above the words "Almighty and everliving God, who hast been pleased to regenerate these thy servants by water and the Holy Ghost, for the forgiveness of all their sins". One cannot say whether this formula will be found completely satisfactory in the light of current discussions of the theology of Baptism and Confirmation, but at least it recognises the existence of a major problem and seeks to deal with it.

We turn from these questions to questions of the structure and content of the revised services. It is not proposed here to trace in any detail the developments and changes which affected the form of the rites of Christian initiation in the West from sub-Apostolic times to the eve of the Reformation.[46] But if we look at one of the Baptismal rites in use in late mediaeval times, for example, that contained in the "Sarum Manual", we can discern a clear pattern much influenced by long-standing precedent.[47] There was, first, an introduction during which the person to be baptised was met at the church door and then solemnly brought to the Font : this part of the service ended in the reading of the Gospel, and was

(46) See L. Duchesne, *Christian Worship*, ch. 9, pp. 292-341 (*tr.* M. L. McClure, London, 5th edition, reprinted 1949): F. Procter and W. H. Frere, *A History of the Book of Common Prayer*, third impression 1905-1949, pp. 557-607; *Liturgy and Worship*, pp. 410-428, 443-457.

(47) The Baptismal rites according to the "Sarum Manual" can be studied in F. E. Brightman, *The English Rite*, Vol. 2, pp. 724*ff*, London, 1915. *Cf.* Procter and Frere, *op. cit.* pp. 564-569.

an echo of the catechumenate, or long period of instruction which the early Church imposed upon candidates for Baptism. Next came a solemn renunciation of Satan and profession of faith, both in three-fold form. Then, after the Blessing of the Water, the Sacrament was administered and the person baptised was received into membership of the Church. There followed prayers and an exhortation concerning Confirmation and the duties of the god-parents. Exorcisms, anointings and other ceremonies marked the progress of the service.

The 1549 services followed this pattern closely, but the Book of 1552, which 1662 followed without much alteration, obscured it. The formal bringing of the candidate into the church was abandoned, and it was ordered that the whole service be performed at the Font. The sequence of the service was further interrupted by the insertion of exhortations of the kind beloved of the Reformers. The revised services have sought to remedy these defects. The solemn leading of the candidate into the church has been restored. The exhortations have either been removed or pruned and reworded. Instead of a service consisting mostly of prayers and exhortations in which the laypeople present have comparatively little part, we now have a service which not only adheres more closely to the pattern of Baptismal rite traditional to the West, but also actively engages the congregation from first to last.

Besides making clearer their traditional pattern and giving them a more liturgical form, the revision attempts to give the Baptismal services more solemnity. We have already discussed the entry of the candidates into the church. One would also point to the form for the Blessing of the Water. In 1662, this is abrupt and bare. In the revised services, the Blessing of the Water is done in Preface form drawn largely from ancient sources, rich in Biblical allusion and altogether a noble example of liturgical language ; the four little prayers which in 1662 introduce the Blessing of the Water now come after it, as they did in the ancient services. Of the ancient ceremonies connected with Baptism it was decided to restore two, the use of which is purely optional and requires the consent of priest and parents. The first is the putting of a white vesture upon the baptized, "as a token of the innocency bestowed upon him by God's grace in this holy Sacrament of Baptism". The second is the giving to a godparent (or to the candidate, if he is an adult)of a lighted candle "as a sign of the light of Christ and of the grace of

Baptism". Both these ceremonies are found in the pre-Reformation rites, and have a long history behind them. In the 7th century, the clothing of candidates in a special robe or "chrysom" was already an established practice in the Western Church, and was retained in England till the Book of 1552. Apparently confined to areas influenced by the Gallican Rite, the giving of a lighted candle or taper is heard of as early as the 4th century and St. Ambrose's episcopate at Milan. The optional use of both ceremonies is permitted by the South African and Indian Books of 1954 and 1951, and by the "Order for Holy Baptism" authorized for experimental use by the Church of South India in October, 1954. The Church in Wales therefore is not alone in allowing the optional and experimental use of these ceremonies; and it will be interesting to see how they stand the test. Here and there, fears have been expressed of their leading to superstition and abuse. More often, practical difficulties involved in their use, particularly when several infants or adults are being baptized together, have been voiced. But there is also a body of opinion which has found both ceremonies meaningful and lovely, and considers that this part of the revised services should have as fair a trial as the rest.[48]

From Baptism we turn to Confirmation. In general, the revision of this service has not been as drastic as that of the Baptismal services. But there have been changes. The 1662 Preface has been removed, and its place is taken by a formal presentation of the candidates to the Bishop on the lines of the Ordination services. The Renewal of the Baptismal vows is completely changed. Instead of the one question by the Bishop to which the candidates answer "I do", we now have a solemn charge to the candidates followed by five questions each requiring its answer, and recalling more explicitly the terms of the Baptismal vows. Apart from the alteration discussed already in the Prayer before the Laying-On of Hands, the rest of the service is substantially the same as that in 1662. It is permitted, however, to sing the "Veni Creator" before the Confirmation proper : and before the Blessing of the candidates a prayer speaking of the privilege of Holy Communion has been inserted. In the interests of correct translation, "manifold" has

(48) Duchesne, *op. cit.* pp. 314, 326 : Procter and Frere *op. cit.* p. 564 (v. especially footnote 4) : article s.n. "Chrysom" in the *Oxford Dictionary of the Christian Church* : S. African Prayer Book, p. 404 : Indian Prayer Book, pp. 285-6 : S. Indian "Order for Holy Baptism", Oxford University Press, Madras, 1955, pp. 9-10.

been altered to "sevenfold" in the Prayer before the Laying-On of Hands. Here as in the Baptismal services, the headings of the various sections make clearer the structure of the rite.

Two other matters need comment. First, a wholesale revision of rubrics has been effected. It is not possible to discuss all the details, but some points may be noted. The new rubrics on the whole make clearer than 1662 did the necessity of Baptism and the obligations it imposes, the persons who may minister it in different circumstances, and several other matters. Existing practice is recognised and regulated, notably in the rubric saying what is to be done when Baptism is administered at Morning and Evening Prayer, or as a separate service. The matter of godparents has been dealt with in a spirit of realism. It will be in many cases a relief to have the minimum number of godparents reduced to two, with permission to a parent to stand godfather or godmother in case of need. On the other hand, it is explicitly stated that godparents are to be "confirmed and practising members of the Church in Wales or of a Church in communion with it" : and it is a gain that the continuing obligations of godparents have been stressed by the requirement that "everyone shall have a godfather or a godmother as a witness of their Confirmation". Other rubrics ought to prove helpful, for example that naming the fourth Sunday after birth as the latest date at which a child should be baptized in normal circumstances. We need some means of combatting the vexatious and quite unnecessary delays in which parents often indulge.

The other question is that of language, The nobility of Cranmerian English, and the pitfalls awaiting revisers of it, were acknowledged early in this study. The Welsh revision has indeed removed archaisms and reworded obscure phrases, but it has striven to preserve Cranmer's standards of liturgical language whether it was a question of revising existing matter or of introducing new matter. The result awaits the test of actual use, as does the Welsh version of the revised services. The day when a Welsh composition passes without a murmur from the "critick lions" will be a day of astonishment indeed. Whatever criticisms there may be of details, it is not unreasonable to hail this version by and large as a fine achievement. Its language is eloquent but firm ; the construction of sentences is clear; and it is a joy indeed to have Welsh versions of services from which there have departed the archaic words, the clumsy phrases, and the obsolete orthography which so often mar the Welsh translation of 1662.

The famous French liturgiologist Anton Baumstark, who died in 1948, began his *Liturgie Comparée* with these words:—"In Liturgy we become aware of the living heart of the Church. In the prayer which ascends to the Throne of God, in the fullness of Sacramental Grace which descends on the common life of the faithful, we are made conscious of the powerful stream of life which pulsates through the Mystical Body of Christ, of the Christ, who, as the Apostle said, 'died once for all', so that 'death shall no longer have dominion over Him'. Never can such living activity be paralysed into the rigour of an immobile and dead formalism"[49]

The Church in Wales in our day, accepting the inescapable logic of these words, has begun the revision of the Book of 1662. Neither the importance nor the crushing complexity of this task could be exaggerated. It will be the prayer of all our faithful people that God Almighty will sustain and bless the work begun, and accept it when complete as the due offering of His ancient Church in Wales. No more than any other body of Christians can that Church make God greater by pleasing Him. But in this and in every other part of her life, she can assuredly make herself less by falling short of her duty towards Him before whom angels and archangels, and the whole company of the redeemed, "rest not day and night, saying

HOLY, HOLY, HOLY, LORD GOD ALMIGHTY WHICH WAS, AND IS, AND IS TO COME"[50]

---

(49) English translation by F. L. Cross, *Comparative Liturgy*, London, 1958, p. 1. This translation was made from the third French edition revised by B. Botte, O.S.B., Editions de Chevetogne, 1953. The book has been universally hailed as a masterpiece and its introduction to English-speaking readers is a happy event in liturgical studies.

(50) Revelation 4. 8.

APPENDIX I

Enactments Defining the Position of the Book of 1662 in the Church in Wales After Disestablishment, The Power of the Governing Body to Revise the Book, and the Procedure Prescribed for Revising It.

A. *The Welsh Church Act, 1914, Section 3, sub-sections 1, 2 and 4 : Ecclesiastical law in the Church in Wales as a contract between her members : power given to modify or alter the ecclesiastical law under the constitution and regulations for the time being of the Church in Wales.*

(1) As from the date of disestablishment . . . the ecclesiastical law of the Church in Wales shall cease to exist as law.

(2) As from the same date the then existing ecclesiastical law and the then existing articles, doctrines, rites, rules discipline and ordinances of the Church of England shall, with and subject to such modification or alteration, if any, as after the passing of this Act may be duly made therein, according to the constitution and regulations for the time being of the Church in Wales, *be binding on members for the time being of the Church in Wales as if they had mutually agreed to be so bound* . . . .

(4) The power of making by such constitution and regulations alterations and modifications in ecclesiastical law shall include the power of altering or modifying such law so far as it is embodied in the Church Discipline Act, 1840, the Public Worship Regulation Act, 1874, the Clergy Discipline Act, 1892, or the Ecclesiastical Dilapidations Acts, 1871 and 1872, *or any other Act of Parliament.*

B. *The Constitution of the Church in Wales, Chapter 2, Section 30 : The acceptance of the 1662 Book by the Governing Body at its creation.*

The Governing Body shall at its creation accept the articles, doctrinal statements, rites, and ceremonies, and, save in so far as they may necessarily be varied by the passing of the Welsh Church Act, 1914, the formularies of the Church of England as accepted by that Church and set forth in or appended to, the Book of Common Prayer, of the Church of England.

C. *The Constitution of the Church in Wales, Schedule to Chapter 7 : Declaration to be made by all admitted to Holy Orders, or appointed to any ecclesiastical office, or licensed as assistant curates, in the Church in Wales.*

(1) I, J . . . . S . . . . , do solemnly make the following declaration. I assent to the Thirty-nine Articles of Religion, and to the Book of Common Prayer, and of Ordering of Bishops, Priests, and Deacons; I believe the doctrine as therein set forth to be agreeable to the Word of God, and in Public Prayer and Administration of the Sacraments I will use the form in the said Book prescribed, and none other, except so far as shall be ordered by lawful authority.

D. *The Constitution of the Church in Wales, Chapter 2, Sections 34-38 : Power of the Governing Body to make alterations in articles, doctrinal statements, rites, ceremonies, and formularies : Bill procedure leading to the promulgation of Canons.*

34

The Governing Body shall have power to make alterations in articles, doctrinal statements, rites, ceremonies, and formularies, provided that no

52

alteration shall be made except by a Bill as hereinafter set forth, backed and introduced in the Governing Body by a majority of the Order of the Bishops, unless such alteration shall have been accepted and assented to by the Church of England, in which event a Bill as hereinafter set forth may be backed and introduced in the Governing Body by any ten members thereof.

35

Any proposed scheme within the meaning of section 31 hereof, and any proposal to alter, amend, or abrogate sections 33 or 40 or this present section, and any proposal concerning faith, discipline, or ceremonial, or concerning any article, doctrinal statement, rites, ceremonies or formularies of the Church in Wales, shall be introduced and enacted by the procedure hereinafter set out with regard to Bills.

36

A Bill shall be read a first time without debate and then be printed and circulated with the names of its backers, who, except in the cases provided for in section 34, shall be any two or more members of the Governing Body. It shall then be set down for debate in the Governing Body upon its principles and a vote shall be taken upon the question whether it shall be read a second time. If a majority of the members of the Governing Body present are in favour of the Bill being read a second time, a day for the Committee stage, after the expiration of a period of twelve months then next, whether in the same or the ensuing Governing Body, shall be fixed by the Chairman for the consideration thereof.

37

For the purpose of procedure under the Committee stage of a Bill, a member shall be appointed by the Governing Body to act as Chairman of Committee, and when so appointed shall continue to act as Chairman of Committee during the continuance of the Session unless the Governing Body shall decide otherwise.

38

After such further consideration in Committee, the Bill shall be reported to the Governing Body, and the votes of each Order taken thereon separately. If the Bill is passed by a two-thirds majority of the members present and voting of each of the three Orders, the President shall promulgate it as a canon of the Church in Wales, and it shall thenceforth be a law of the Church in Wales and binding on all the members thereof.

Provided always that the Order of the Bishops shall not vote till after the declaration of the votes of the other two Orders. Upon such declaration of votes the Order of the Bishops may, if they think fit, retire for private debate, and announce the result of their voting at such later time during that Session of the Governing Body as they shall think fit.

53

APPENDIX II

Canons Relating to Public Worship promulgated by the Governing Body Since Disestablishment : The Calendar of Welsh Saints.

A. *The Permissive Use of the New Lectionary in the Church in Wales (Easter,* 1924).

WHEREAS new Tables of Lessons have received the approval of the Convocations of Canterbury and York, and an Act, known as the Revised Tables of Lessons Measure, having the new Tables of Lessons appended to it, has been passed by the National Assembly of the Church of England, and passed by each House of Parliament under the procedure laid down in the Church of England Assembly (Powers) Act, 1919, and received the Royal Assent on 4th August, 1922.

AND WHEREAS, by the Revised Tables of Lessons Measure the new Tables of Lessons are authorised as from Advent Sunday, 1922, as an optional alternative Lectionary in the Church of England.

THAT the Governing Body resolve that, under Section 36, Chapter II, of the Constitution of the Church in Wales, the said New Tables of Lessons be authorised as an optional alternative Lectionary in the Church in Wales as from the Advent Sunday next following the passing of this Bill by the Governing Body.

PROVIDED that when the new Tables of Lessons have once been adopted in any Church, the same Tables shall there be continuously followed at least until the end of the Ecclesiastical Year.

B. *For Allowing Deacons or Priests to be made and Ordained upon the Saturdays in the Ember Weeks (September,* 1933).

Whereas in former days it was customary and lawful for Deacons or Priests to be made and ordained upon the Saturdays within *Jejunia quatuor temporum,* commonly called Ember weeks.

And whereas it is expedient in these latter days to allow and permit Deacons or Priests to be made and ordained upon the Saturdays within the Ember weeks.

Be it hereby enacted that after the passing of this Bill it shall be lawful within and throughout the Province of Wales for Deacons or Priests to be made and ordained upon the Saturdays within the Ember weeks aforesaid, besides and as well as upon the days appointed and allowed in the Form and manner of making, Ordaining and Consecrating of Bishops, Priests and Deacons, contained within or annexed unto the Book of Common Prayer.

C. *Experimental Use of Proposed Revisions of the Book of Common Prayer, Provisionally Approved by the Bench of Bishops. (September,* 1956).

Whereas at its meeting on 13th April, 1950 the Governing Body of the Church in Wales requested His Grace the Archbishop to appoint a Commission called "The Standing Liturgical Commission" whose duty should be to submit from time to time recommendations to the Bench of Bishops concerning such amendments as might be necessary or desirable in the Church's law of worship. And whereas such a Commission has been set up and will submit from time to time recommendations to the Bench of Bishops for revisions of parts of the Book of Common Prayer. And whereas it its provided by Chapter II of the Constitution that the Governing Body shall have power to make alterations in the Book of Common Prayer provided that no alteration shall be made except by a Bill backed and introduced in the Governing Body by a majority of the Order of the Bishops unless such alteration shall have been accepted and assented to by the Church of England in which event a Bill may be backed and introduced in the Governing Body by any ten members thereof. And whereas in the opinion of the Bench of Bishops it may be desirable that before a Bill for the revision of a part or parts of the Book of Common Prayer is submitted by the Bench of Bishops for the consideration of the Governing Body the proposed revision should be used experimentally in the parishes for a limited period.

Be it hereby enacted that:—

1. A diocesan bishop shall have power to authorise for experimental use in the churches within his diocese any proposed revisions of a part or parts of the Book of Common Prayer which have been provisionally approved by the Bench of Bishops, provided that the said authorisation shall be for a limited period not exceeding ten years, and provided that the Governing Body shall have assented to the experimental use of the proposed revision without alteration.

2. A diocesan bishop shall not take action under Clause I hereof until after the next meeting of the Governing Body following the circulation to the members of the Governing Body of printed copies of the proposed revision.

D. *The Calendar of Welsh Saints* (*September*, 1944)

Ionawr *Century*

24	Catwg, *i.e.*, Cadog (Cadoc)	Abad	Cyffesor	End of 5th
29	Gildas	Abad	Cyffesor	c. 540

Chwefror

1	Ffraid Leian (Bride)	Gwyryf	Abades	6th
9	Teilo	Esgob	Cyffesor	Early 6th

Mawrth

1	Dewi (David)	Esgob Nawdd Sant Cymru.	Cyffesor	End of 5th and beginning of 6th
5	Non, Mam Dewi (Nonnita, Mother of David)			5th
17	Padrig (Patrick)	Esgob	Cyffesor	5th
29	Gwynllyw Filwr (Woolo)	Brenin	Cyffesor	5th

Ebrill

7	Brynach	Cyffesor		6th
15	Padarn	Esgob	Cyffesor	6th
21	Beuno	Abad	Cyffesor	6th-7th

Mai

* 1	Asaff (Asaph)	Esgob	Cyffesor	Late 6th

Mehefin

22	Alban	Merthyr		c. 300

*Transferred from May 1st to May 5th.

Gorffennaf

1	Iwl ac Aaron (Julius and Aaron.)		Merthyron		*c.* 300
3	Peblig		Cyffesor		End of 4th
28	Samson		Esgob	Cyffesor	6th
31	GARMON (GERMANUS)		Esgob	Cyffesor	6th

Medi

11	DEINIOL (DANIEL)		Esgob	Cyffesor	6th

Hydref

9	Cynog		Cyffesor	5th

Tachwedd

3	GWENFREWI (WINIFRED)		Gwyryf	Abades	Early 7th
5	Cybi		Abad	Cyffesor	6th
6	ILLTUD		Abad	Cyffesor	5th-6th
8	Tysilio		Abad	Cyffesor	6th
12	HOLL SANT CYMRU (ALL SAINTS OF WALES)				
14	Dyfrig (Dubricius)		Esgob	Cyffesor	5th-6th
22	Peulin (Paulinus)		Abad	Cyffesor	6th

NOTES

Where possible, the English equivalent is given in brackets.

The date of the Saint's day, set down, is, in each case, based upon the oldest existing Kalendars (*Cf.* Baring Gould and Fisher, Vol. I, pages 70 and ff.).

November 12th is suggested for HOLL SAINT CYMRU (ALL SAINTS OF WALES), being outside the Octave of ALL SAINTS, and also the first available date.

It is suggested that, when the Festival of Dewi (David) falls outside Lent, the Octave of the Festival of Dewi should be observed throughout the Province, in view of his being the National Patron Saint.

It is also suggested that the Octaves of the Saints of the first rank should be observed in each Diocese, or Parish, of which they are respectively Patron Saints.

(With the correction of one obvious printing error, the text of the Calendar given here is that printed in the Governing Body Minutes for 27th and 28th September, 1944. Non, however comes on March 3rd in the text given in *Emynau'r Eglwys*, full edition, 1951, p. 776.)

APPENDIX III

List of Members of the Standing Liturgical Commission.

The Very Reverend Eryl S. Thomas, Dean of Llandaff (*Chairman*).

The Very Reverend H. J. Charles, Dean of St. Asaph.

The Very Reverend R. E. Evans, Dean of Monmouth.

The Very Reverend W. E. Jones, Dean of Brecon.

The Venerable J. Richards Pugh, Archdeacon of Carmarthen.

The Venerable R. Ward, Archdeacon of Cardigan.

The Reverend Canon M. E. Davies, Vicar of St. Mary's, Abergavenny.

The Reverend Canon W. L. Harris, Vicar of Pendoylan.

The Reverend Canon W. U. Jacob, Vicar of St. Peter's, Carmarthen.

The Reverend Chancellor N. G. Matthews, Rector of St. Fagans with Llanillterne

The Reverend Canon W. J. Rees, Vicar of Welshpool.

The Reverend Canon J. H. Williams, Vicar of Caernarvon.

The Reverend Euros Bowen, Vicar of Llangywair.

The Reverend D. G. G. Davies, Curate-in-Charge of West Cross, Swansea.

The Reverend F. W. G. Griffiths, Rector of Llanelwedd.

The Reverend W. D. Parry, Vicar of Llandinam.

The Reverend O. G. Rees, Warden of St. Michael's College, Llandaff.

Mr. Aneirin Talfan Davies, Assistant Head of Programmes, Welsh Region, B.B.C.

Mr. Charles A. Gladstone, Chairman of the Representative Body of the Church in Wales.

Dr. Evan J. Jones, formerly Professor of Education, University College of Swansea.

Captain N. G. Garnons Williams, R.N. (*ret.*), Justice of the Peace for the County of Brecon.

Mr. R. R. Wilson, Archbishop's Registrar, Lay Secretary of the Governing Body and Secretary of the Representative Body of the Church in Wales.

The Reverend E. O. T. Lewis, Vicar of Llanblethian with Cowbridge (*Honorary Secretary*).

PRINTED BY
D. BROWN AND SONS, LTD.,
COWBRIDGE, GLAMORGAN.